Maybe Luck Isn't Just Chance

MAYBE LUCK ISN'T JUST CHANCE

RUTH LIEPMAN

Translated by John A. Broadwin

With a Historical Postscript by Inge Marssolek

NORTHWESTERN UNIVERSITY PRESS

Evanston, Illinois

Northwestern University Press
Evanston, Illinois 60208-4210

Originally published in German under the title *Vielleicht ist Glück nicht nur Zufall*. Copyright © 1993 by Verlag Kiepenheüer & Witsch, Köln. English translation copyright © 1997 by Northwestern University Press. Published 1997 by arrangement with Verlag Kiepenheuer & Witsch, Köln. All rights reserved.

Printed in the United States of America

ISBN 0-8101-1294-9 (cloth)
ISBN 0-8101-1295-7 (paper)

Library of Congress Cataloging-in-Publication Data

Liepman, Ruth, 1909–
  [Vielleicht ist Glück nicht nur Zufall. English]
  Maybe luck isn't just chance / Ruth Liepman ; translated by John A. Broadwin ; with a historical postscript by Inge Marssolek.
    p. cm. — (Jewish lives)
  Includes bibliographical references.
  ISBN 0-8101-1294-9 (cloth : alk. paper). — ISBN 0-8101-1295-7 (paper : alk. paper)
  1. Liepman, Ruth, 1909– . 2. Literary agents—Germany—Biography. I. Title. II. Series.
PN163.L5413 1998
070.5'2—dc21
[B]   97-39708
                                                 CIP

�֎

Contents

❀

Author's Note

For a number of years I refused to publish my memoirs in the form of a book. My decision to do so now at the age of eighty-three was prompted by the fact that there are no longer many witnesses left from the generation born around 1910 who lived through two world wars and experienced firsthand the collapse of entire empires. This book about my life emerged during the course of my many conversations with Helge Malchow.

Ruth Liepman, Spring 1992

Maybe Luck Isn't Just Chance

✿

Introduction

Whenever I think back, I keep recalling an incident that took place in the spring of 1933. Adolf Hitler had been Reich chancellor for several weeks, and it was open season on the opposition, that is, the Left. Many of my friends and acquaintances had already been arrested. I had just turned twenty-four and was finishing my in-service training in preparation for taking the second state examination in law. Whether I could take the exam and go on to practice was very much in doubt. On a sunny spring afternoon I was sitting at a round table beneath a fruit tree in full bloom at a farmstead in Prasdorf near Kiel. Cake and coffee were served. However, the reason for our visit was most serious. After the mass arrests that had taken place over the past few weeks, Hans Kippenberger (1898–1937)—a leading functionary of the KPD (Kommunistische Partei Deutschlands, or Communist Party of Germany) and Reichstag deputy—and his wife, Thea, were forced to go into hiding. And we had to find a place for their four-year-old daughter, if only to protect the Kippenbergers from being blackmailed by threats to harm the child. My boyfriend Werner Bockelmann (1907–70) helped find a hiding place on a farm. The farmer's wife—tall, blond, and attractive—was one Lili Arp, the mother-in-law of Bock-elmann's brother Rudi. She was prepared to take the child into her home. All of us—Werner, Lili, her son, and a few of their friends—sat around a big table watching the little girl playing in the meadow.

Prasdorf, incidentally, was one of the last enclaves of

matriliny in Germany. Inheritance was through the widow or eldest child—even if the child were female—and not through the eldest son, as elsewhere in the region. Because of this special instance of descent through the female line, Lili Arp had become the head of the household. Whether this is still the case, I don't know. In any event, the fact that Lili Arp was in charge of the farm (she did a splendid job of managing it, by the way) was certainly a factor in her readiness to assume responsibility for the care of the child. She realized that her actions were not without danger.

The reason that this particular incident, which goes back almost sixty years, comes to mind may be connected to the fact that it contains many of the themes that run like a red thread through my life: the atmosphere of constant danger and, at the same time, the friends who were always there when we in the resistance worked together and succeeded in actively opposing the Nazis; the illegal acts in which I quite matter-of-factly engaged without giving much thought to their motives; my naive faith at the time in the Communist Party; and, last but not least, Prasdorf's verdant tranquillity and my relationship to Werner Bockelmann, with whom I was in love—never dreaming that this love could be destroyed as a result of what was to occur during the Nazi period.

✿

Childhood

My first memory was a happy one. I had just learned to walk and was toddling along, as small children do, when all of a sudden a black animal came toward me. It must have been a dog or a lamb or a goat, a big black one. Though I wasn't afraid, I fell over backward, landing on my bottom with my legs outstretched, hoping to prevent it from knocking me over first. My reaction may have been motivated by a touch of fear, but it was also combined with a feeling of curiosity and a sense of having overcome a difficult situation.

The incident took place in Polch near Koblenz in the Eifel* region, where I was born in 1909. My father, Theo Lilienstein, had established his first practice there after graduating from medical school. Otherwise I have no memory of that village in the Eifel. Later, my father would tell me how he treated the village children for diphtheria and how he would be asked to come to a farm when a child was choking. He told me how he would heat a kitchen knife [for cauterization] and make an incision to open the child's windpipe. Of course, he was also expected to give advice whenever a cow or a horse fell ill. He was a dedicated doctor, trusted by all, accepted as a matter of course, and respected—even though he was Jewish.

My father was the scion of a Jewish family from Usingen in the Taunus,† not far from Frankfurt am Main, where my

---

*Plateau region of western Germany, lying between the Rhine, the Mosel, and the Luxembourg and Belgian frontiers.—Trans.

†Wooded highland of Germany, extending across parts of the *Länder* (states) of Hesse and Rhineland–Palatinate.

grandparents, my cousins, and their dog Polly lived. There were sacks of grain stored all over the courtyard of their house. Like many Jews in small towns, my grandparents were feed and grain merchants. Being the eldest son, my father attended university. The family had a large house on Unter-gasse that had a room reserved exclusively for the storage of baked goods. My grandmother baked every day, and even now I can recall the smell of freshly baked plum cake. My cousin Hilde and I were allowed to go anywhere in the house, even to the pantries where apples and potatoes were stored for the winter. The aroma of apples and potatotes pervaded the entire house. My grandmother was a loving woman with rosy cheeks who looked after the whole family, especially the grandchildren. Nothing tasted better than a piece of bread from a freshly baked loaf spread with homemade butter.

I can even remember my great-grandfather. He would sit in a rocking chair wearing a skullcap, put me on his lap, and rock me back and forth. His black cap was embroidered and flat on top.

My mother's parents lived in Bad Ems,* not very far away. My mother was an exceptionally beautiful woman. In fact, she was once courted by the crown prince. Years later, in our attic in Hamburg, I found the paper used to wrap a bouquet he had presented her with. The inscription read: "As a token of my affection. For the most beautiful woman in Bad Ems." I had a funny feeling when I touched the frilly paper. I had no idea what "token of affection" meant.

My mother's family were also members of the Jewish mid-dle class. My parents were cousins. My grandparents in Bad Ems had a couple of shoe stores and lived on Braubachstrasse in a big house near a hill. There was a magnificent garden behind the house. My female cousin and I used to pick wild strawberries there. When strawberries came into season, you could smell them all over the house. The hill behind the house was more important to us children than the house itself. On the other hand, the bathroom had colored *Jugendstil* tiles, and

---

*A spa town. —Trans.

it was hard for me to pull myself away, because I was always fascinated by the stories depicted on the tiles.

During the tourist season my grandparents rented out rooms to people taking the waters at Bad Ems. In this way, they supplemented their income from the two shoe stores. We children had fun packing and unpacking the shoes and trying on pairs that were several sizes too large for us.

My grandparents on both sides of my family were practicing Jews. They helped support poorer members of the Jewish community, inviting them to celebrate the Sabbath with them. Although they continued to observe the Sabbath, my parents had ceased to do so. Whenever we were told that my grandmother from Bad Ems would be coming to visit us, my mother made sure that everything in the house was kosher, just as my grandmother expected it to be.

My parents were not religious Jews. From the beginning, it was my father who figured most prominently in introducing me to the idea of rational thinking. He sought to explain the world without reference to God. However, even though religion did not play a part in our lives, we always referred to ourselves as Jews and considered ourselves Jewish. I felt especially Jewish on the major Jewish holidays after their meaning had been explained to me. During Passover we read the Haggadah aloud at home, usually with guests present. I very much loved the story of the Jewish exodus from Egypt. When I was a child, I was allowed to ask the question "Why is this night different from all other nights?" The response was the story of Passover.

After the first few years in Polch, my father developed a specialty in dermatology, traveling from city to city — Cologne, Berlin, Hamburg — and always taking my mother and me along with him. I remember seeing the cathedral in Cologne and taking part in the carnival festivities. I went as Little Red Riding Hood and wore a little red velvet skirt, jacket, and cap.

In Berlin we lived on Mommsenstrasse. I had a black velvet coat with a light blue lining. The lining was much prettier than the coat, and I was always turning it inside out, because I delighted in showing it off.

My "bad" grandmother from Bad Ems came to see us once. In contrast to my grandmother from Usingen, I always regarded her as an especially severe person. One day we were walking past a shop with a red bow in the window that I simply had to have for my hair. I had long black braids and stood in front of the shop crying because she would not buy me the bow. She finally relented, though not without grumbling. But I ended up with the bow in my hair.

The family finally settled in Hamburg. I must have been four or five years old at the time. My father opened his first practice there before World War I, specializing in venereal and skin diseases. He had studied at the well-known medical school in Würzburg and had an abiding attachment to that city. He was a member of the Jewish fencing fraternity VEDA in Würzburg and even had a fencing scar on his cheek as proof of his bravery and—like many other Jews of the day—of his German nationalism. His fraternity brother and best friend during this period, Dr. Goldschmidt, nicknamed Golo, lived in Hamburg, and I'm sure that was one of the reasons Father decided to settle there.

We lived on Schulterblatt at first, a very lively street, in an apartment on the border between Hamburg and Altona. There was a movie theater across the street on the corner. In those days there was something risqué about a movie theater; a decent neighborhood would never have tolerated one. In fact, I don't recall my parents ever having gone to the movies. You went to the theater, or to a concert. In my father's case, business and pleasure went hand in hand, for he was often on duty in the theater as the so-called theater physician, receiving two free tickets in exchange. When Mummy didn't go, I was permitted to accompany him, especially to the opera. From time to time, members of the family enjoyed giving amateur musical concerts at home.

When I think of my parents back then, I recall a time during the First World War when my father came home on leave for a brief visit. I overheard my parents talking. Children are aware of everything. I was still little and slept in a crib in my parents' bedroom. Father had given the head nurse in the military hospital an innocent kiss and told Mother about it. I heard her crying; then I began to cry too. My father calmed her. I was confused, not knowing whose side to take, though I tended to sympathize with my mother. It was the only problem I ever encountered in my parents' marriage. My father and mother were and remained a happily married couple as long as they lived. My mother was in charge of day-to-day activities. Father worked in his practice, delivered lectures, and wrote articles for medical journals.

My father wanted me to become a doctor from the time I was a small child, so one day he took me with him to the Institute of Tropical Medicine. We were shown a dog whose brain had been invaded by a tropical insect, causing the poor creature to turn round and round in circles. When the dog was given an injection, I fainted . . .

The words *big city* meant, among other things, that I had to go with my nanny to the zoo or the botanical gardens. I remember the zoo quite well, especially the aviary, because my nanny was having a fling with the keeper in charge of the birdcages. All of a sudden I began receiving gifts of the loveliest feathers. Once, the two of them were fussing so much that they neglected to notice that the zoo had closed. So we had to exit through the zoo director's house and arrived home late. My mother was very distraught and wanted to know what had happened. I snitched, and the nanny was dismissed.

I was happy, though, because her dismissal solved my biggest problem. I never felt like eating, and the nanny used to wedge me between her legs and force-feed me as though I were a duck or a goose and she a farmer stuffing food down my gullet. She would stick a piece of bread in my mouth and say: "You're going to swallow this or else." I hated that bread so much that I wanted to spit it out.

I always ate very slowly, probably to irk my mother. So a small plate of hot water was placed beside my food to keep it warm. My meals were an ordeal for everyone. I always thought if I had children someday, I wouldn't force them to eat anything. The struggle over food ended when my brother, ten years my junior, was born. He immediately became the object of my love, and I sought to protect him from my strong-willed mother. I am sure she always had my best interest at heart and her intentions were the best, but from the outset I made an effort to assert myself and stand up to her. My mother thought I would die if I didn't eat. When I attended Dr. Loewenberg's high school for girls, I always tried to be last in line whenever we students linked arms to form up, so that I could secretly pitch my school lunch unnoticed into the wastepaper basket. I was only able to do this if I managed to end up last in line. I was simply uninterested in eating.

One day my mother found out what I had been doing. She asked what I had put on my bread that day. Staring into space, I answered, "Cheese." "Cheese," she said suspiciously. "What you mean to say is that you didn't eat your bread." Thus the truth emerged that I had been throwing away the wartime ration of bread that my mother had been denying herself. Though I had a guilty conscience, I simply couldn't get that bread down.

Even though I ate practically nothing, I was still quite robust and strong. Eating always meant feeding to me, and feeding meant fights with Mother. When I was a very small child, I would be seated in a high chair and fed little pieces of doughnut. Mummy would tell me stories. I would keep the food in my mouth until my cheeks bulged. Mother would say: "If you don't swallow, I won't tell you the rest of the story." I would look at her and say: "If you don't tell me the rest of the story, I'll never swallow again." She continued telling the story—it was a major victory for me over my mother. The combination of my mother's solicitude and my desire to be independent gave rise to real hostility.

The Loewenberg School on Johannesallee was quite a distance from home, a forty-minute walk each way. My mother used to take me there and pick me up every day. She wouldn't allow to me walk alone, regardless of how much I pleaded with her. Still, she was a charming, playful woman. One day, for instance, I came home to find her under a table playing with my brother's electric model train . . .

Here's another little anecdote. I once had an inflammation of the nail bed. Mother and I were living alone at home. Daddy was away at war. She had great confidence in Dr. Goldschmidt; his office was on the corner of Klosterallee and Isestrasse. Golo said to me, "I have to do something to your finger. It won't hurt." I believed him. In fact, it hurt like the dickens. I was furious that he had tricked me. He tried to calm me by giving me some chocolate, a rarity during the war. I threw it on the floor in front of him. That was my first great disappointment in people.

I was always a good student. Fräulein Kassel, our home-room teacher, took us through the multiplication table. She wanted us to write down our answers on our slates, after which she would put the correct answers on the blackboard. Students with the correct answers were supposed to raise their hand. Though I kept coming up with the right answers, I had a tendency to transpose the digits when writing them down, for example, 23 instead of 32. So I would erase them and raise my hand anyway. When Fräulein Kassel spotted me, she said, "You're lying. I saw you change your answer." It was impossible for me to make her believe that I had multiplied correctly but written the answer down wrong. There was an awful brouhaha. First, I was sent to see the principal, who told me, "You will stand under the clock for half an hour." The reason for this punishment was that every child had to walk past the clock. However, I refused to do so: "I didn't lie. I always got the answers right, I just wrote them down wrong." He called my mother. Indignant, I told her the whole story. Mother cried, but she went to the principal and defended me: "Ruth doesn't lie. She's a saucy little thing, but she doesn't tell lies." And that was the truth: I never recall telling a lie when I was little. I'm sure Mummy was despondent, but she stood by me nevertheless.

I had early developed a naive but powerful sense of justice, which was encouraged by my family. For example, my father treated many more patients in the national health-care program and patients on welfare than he did private-care patients, which was anything but routine in those days. There was a well-appointed waiting room for "ordinary" patients; private-care patients had a special place in the entrance hall where the one advantage they had was quicker access to the doctor.

My father explained to me more than once how important it was to treat patients in the national health-care program exactly the same as other patients. I asked him what the difference was, and he replied, "Private-care patients pay out of pocket, others pay through the national-health care program—that's all. I treat everyone equally to the best of my ability." I learned early from my father that money was not the measure of a human being's worth.

I met my boyfriends and girlfriends in the "Blau-Weiss" ("Blue and White") Jewish youth league.[*] It was here that we gained an awareness of being Jewish, of being different from other children, both in and out of school. We read works by Jewish writers, and we had an opportunity to learn Hebrew. However, I wasn't particularly interested in learning Hebrew. Palestine played a big part in the league's activities. A number of the members talked about their desire to emigrate there.

Though no one called me names then because I was Jewish, anti-Semitism was clearly present. On the way to school, for instance, we passed houses that had flyers stuck to the walls with slogans such as "Kill the Jews" or lines from an anti-Semitic song of the time: "When Jew blood spurts from our knives, how much better off we'll be." We would always pull the flyers off.

My parents didn't want me to join "Blau-Weiss," but I was determined to become a member. Part of the reason was that I

---

[*]Blau-Weiss, founded in 1912, was the first Jewish youth movement in Germany. It initiated a Zionist program, basing its organizational structure on that of the German youth movement.—Trans.

was an only child and wanted very much to play with other children. One of my classmates, Edith, sponsored me. Most of the students at the girls' high school were Jewish, as was the principal, Dr. Loewenberg. My parents were sorry that I had early made a decision not to accompany them on their Sunday constitutional. I wanted to go hiking with people my own age. I was infatuated with one of our group leaders. He was a slender, lively boy who could dance the hora and sing Hebrew and Yiddish songs. It was in the "Blau-Weiss" that I for the first time heard about a certain "big shot" from Breslau—a particularly bright young man who was greatly respected in the youth movement. His name was Norbert Elias,[*] and I was to meet him for the first time half a century later.

---

[*]Norbert Elias (1897–1990), a sociologist who described the growth of civilization in Western Europe as a complex evolutionary process, most notably in his principal work, *The Civilizing Process: The History of Manners.*—Trans.

❧

The First World War

Like many other German Jews, my father immediately vol-
unteered for military service; he was just sorry that it
took so long for him to be inducted. As a physician, he was
ultimately assigned to the military hospitals at Altbreisach and
Neubreisach near Freiburg. Even though I was only five
years old, I was well aware of what was happening. When I
thought about Father going off to war and realized that people were shooting at one another, I wondered what was going
to become of us, and I was afraid. Later during the war, my
father's aide, a gunner named Bender, gave me a scrapbook
entitled "Father at War."

Officers were permitted to take their wives and children
with them for a time. That's how I ended up at the convent
school in Breisach in the middle of the war. I was seven when
my mother and I went to Breisach in 1916. I remember the
convent perfectly—the nuns, their habits, even the surrounding Alsatian villages. About a year later we were evacuated,
since the area had become a war zone.

The school in Breisach was a convent school run by the
Ursulines. I felt very much at home there. Most of the students were Catholic, of course, though there were Jewish and
Protestant girls as well. Although each group received separate religious instruction, I attended all the religion classes,
and on Sunday I sometimes even went to church.

I was the school pet, pampered by nuns and parents alike,
even though I couldn't speak Alsatian German. The other
children made fun of me at first when I told them about
Hamburg and its port (*Hafen* in German), because *Hafen* in

their dialect was close to their word for chamber pot (*Häfele*).

All the children went to school barefoot, and I soon followed suit—one more difference from life in the big city. During this period we lived in a fifth-floor apartment on Marktplatz [market square] in Alt-Breisach. There was a lumber store on Marktplatz that used the square for drying freshly cut boards. The boards were stacked up high and were ideal for playing seesaw. I would often rock back and forth on them. We children were warned that the boards would collapse if we continued to play on them. However, it wasn't until the whole pile came crashing down one day that we stopped.

I saw the war as it was reflected in the faces of the many sick and wounded in the military hospital. The wounded soldiers all knew me as the doctor's daughter.

There were frequent air-raid alerts. When the sirens wailed, we were supposed to head for the basement shelter. Once, I was playing with a neighbor child and completely forgot about my mother. She was in the apartment upstairs and didn't always hear the siren. The other children and I went down to the air-raid shelter. After the all-clear signal, I emerged and went back upstairs. My mother asked me where I had been and why I was coming home so late. "There was an air-raid alert," I said. "And you didn't try to get me? You didn't think about your mother?" She was right, I hadn't. I was more interested in playing. I had a guilty conscience but had no idea how to make amends.

Bender, the gunner whom I mentioned earlier, was one of the wounded soldiers. He tried to teach me how to ice skate on the frozen Rhine River. Naturally, I immediately broke my leg in the process of learning.

I clearly remember the villages in Alsace. We used to get butter from the farmers in Alsace as well as in the Kaiserstuhl region.* Occasionally, when my father had time, we went on

---

*A volcanic massif on the right bank of the Rhine.—Trans.

outings, to the Feldberg* near Freiburg, for instance. On one of those outings the snow was so deep, he had to carry me on his shoulder. He got a hernia as a result . . .

This period of the war has remained very much in my memory, mainly because of the kindness shown me by the sisters in the Ursuline convent, the nuns with the cone-shaped coifs. Ever since that time I wanted to revisit Breisach.

Forty years later, after the end of World War II, my husband, Heinz Liepman (1905–66), and I actually did go back to see whether the school still existed, how the nuns had fared during the Nazi era, and if Sister Benedicta (my homeroom teacher) and Sister Angelika were still there.

It was a hot summer's day, and I had some trepidations about our get-together. We sat waiting on a sofa covered in green velvet in an old-fashioned *Jugendstil* room inside the convent. My teacher Sister Angelika entered—she had become a sister superior in the meantime. I remember that as a child I was always struck by the fact that the name *Angelika* meant "angel." And that's exactly what she was—an angel. When Sister Angelika came into the room, I could see that she had become quite the little old mother. She still had a twinkle in her eye, though, and the first words out of her mouth were, "My, if it isn't little Ruthie." I had attended school in Breisach for a very brief time, but Sister Angelika remembered everything that had happened in class forty years earlier, including the pranks I had played. My husband was quite taken aback.

Sister Angelika proceeded to tell us what a difficult time she had had during the Nazi period. There had been numerous attempts to shut down the convent; however, none of them had succeeded. The nuns had become indispensable because of their role as teachers and because of the other activities they performed in Breisach. As our visit was ending, Sister Angelika said to me, "You know a lot of young people, don't you? If you ever come across any who you feel could adapt to life in a convent, we'd be more than pleased to accept them. We're not getting any new blood . . . " Then she led us into the garden and gave us a huge basket of fruit.

*The highest mountain of the Black Forest.—Trans.

When Breisach became a war zone, my mother and I were forced to leave, and my father was sent to the front, where he was wounded in the well-known battle for the Hartmannweilerkopf near the Swiss border. Having received no word from him for some time after the battle, Mother became desperate. When I once quite innocently suggested that she look at the list of those missing in action, she immediately burst into tears, even though I wasn't thinking that anything serious had happened to him. We later heard that he had been wounded in the thigh. He was awarded the decoration for soldiers wounded by enemy action.

Mummy and I returned to Hamburg, but living alone with me was too hard on her. So we moved in with my grandparents in Bad Ems, where I transferred to another school. All I remember about the school is that it was the first and last place I ever got rapped on the knuckles—for mimicking a woman teacher. I also had to quickly learn to speak another—third—dialect.

❁

Hamburg and the Lichtwark School

No sooner had we arrived in Hamburg—my father was there, too—than the November Revolution [1918] broke out. One day during the upheaval, my mother and I went to the Colonnades,[*] where my father maintained an afternoon practice. Even now there are doctors who, in addition to their main practice elsewhere in the city, have a kind of secondary practice in the Colonnades. We were on our way to pick up my father after work, when gunfire suddenly erupted. Mother grabbed me by the arm and pulled me into a doorway. I still recall the incident whenever I walk through the Colonnades in Hamburg. There was a great deal of noise, and I was frightened. It was the sound of organized marchers, the tramp of demonstrating workers and soldiers. My father, who, like many others, had returned from the war a disillusioned man, came down on the side of the revolutionaries. He said that the war was so senseless and so horrible that one had no choice but to oppose it. He was a very open-minded, liberal person. Though I was only nine years old in 1918, I was aware that it was the workers who were rebelling.

My father immediately reopened his practice on Schulterblatt. Later, when conditions improved for us, we moved to a house on Sophienallee. It wasn't a big house, so father put a Latin saying on the outside: *parva sed apta mihi* (little but just right for me). He continued to maintain his practice on Schulterblatt.

---

[*] A network of arcades with elegant shops.—Trans.

My brother Manfred was born in 1918, and my youngest brother, Wolfgang Robert, ten years later, in 1928. I was nineteen at the time, and he could have been my son. Rather innocently I told my mother, "If you die giving birth, I'll take the child." I thought this would reassure her . . .

Subsequently, I returned to the Loewenberg School. The principal, Dr. Loewenberg, was a Hamburg poet, a friend of Richard Dehmel, Detlev von Liliencron, and other contemporary Hamburg writers. He was also an engaging, middle-aged grandfather and Reform Jew. The classrooms were decorated everywhere with paintings depicting scenes from fairy tales, a unique practice in its day. I felt very much at home there and always liked school. An institution exclusively for women, the Loewenberg School—or to be more exact, my Latin teacher, the elder Loewenberg's son—was responsible for my attending the Lichtwark School, which turned out to be an experience that changed my life.

During the Weimar period the Lichtwark School in Hamburg was a kind of experiment in education. Today it is properly considered an important educational institution of the time, and a great deal has been written about it since.[*] Its motto was: a school that makes you hungry but doesn't fill you up.

What we learned there helped make us knowledgeable individuals who were prepared to become socially and politically involved and to fight for change. Nowadays people might call it an alternative school. Many modern teaching methods were tested there after World War I. My girlfriend Ruth Tassoni (b. 1908), who was half a grade behind me, even recalls universities refusing to accept graduates of the school. Once, when Ruth—who later became a writer—wrote a paper on Lessing at the University of Hamburg, a professor commented that it was typical of Lichtwark graduates to write about Lessing. Even in those days the Lichtwark School was coeducational,

---

[*]See, for example, *Die Lichtwarkschule: Idee und Gestalt* (Hamburg: Selbstverlag des Arbeitskreises Lichtwarkschule, 1979).

and some of the students were on a first-name basis with their homeroom teachers.

A good many homeroom teachers spoke openly with us—we were adolescents, after all—about the problems of puberty. Though they were all equally broad-minded, the teachers managed to make each of their homeroom classes unique. We even discussed current events during class. I still remember the execution of Sacco and Vanzetti in 1927 and how we asked our history teacher for more information about the case. When the school was founded, that is, before I enrolled, they didn't even have classes, just so-called special interest groups. Though this eventually changed, the school continued to be unconventional. We performed skits on political themes and published a school newspaper, *Der Querkopf* (The contrarian), which I helped edit.

Being my bullheaded self, I managed to gain admission to the Lichtwark School over the objection of my parents. They would have preferred for me to get my high school diploma from the well-known and prestigious Hamburg School for Girls (Hamburger Mädchenschule). I never regretted having attended the Lichtwark School. The level of instruction was high, but what we learned most was how to work independently, that is, where to find resources, how to study, how to use a library. To repeat, what was most important was being educated to think for ourselves.

Most of my classmates remained friends for life. Sadly, many of them have died over the years. My best friends, Gerhard and Gertrud Lüdtke, died several years ago in Hamburg. The feelings I have for Hamburg as my hometown derive mainly from the time I went to school there. I'm sure there aren't many people who were as fond of school as we were.

Ruth Tassoni is the last living girlfriend from my school days. She now lives in Bergamo in Northern Italy and has published several volumes of short stories.[*]

---

[*]Ruth Tassoni, *Lichtpunkte: autobiographische Splitter* (Zurich: Pendo, 1990).

There weren't as many Jewish students at the Lichtwark School as there had been at the Loewenberg School. There were five Jewish girls in my class: Miriam Besser, Lisel Abeles, Rosi Mendel, Anni Gottschalk—and me.

It should come as no surprise that most of my classmates developed into very special adults. One of them, Martin Boyken, became the mayor of a town in the Harz mountains. Gerhard Lüdtke, my Hamburg friend of many years, was a literary critic, writer, and artistic director for German television. He suffered greatly during the course of his life. Both he and his wife took part in the Spanish Civil War. Later, he was arrested by the Germans in France and transferred from camp to camp, moving inexorably eastward. He ended up fighting in a penal company on the Russian front, where he ultimately became a prisoner of war of the Soviets. It was years before he was repatriated to Hamburg, after which he suffered bouts of severe depression. Whenever I think about our school, I'm surprised by how courageous the students were and how they struck out in unconventional directions.

I was especially interested in *Kulturgeschichte* (the history of civilization), that is, the study of art, science, history, and religion as they relate to one another. To this day I consider the unified approach to the study of civilization a model of scholarly inquiry, as opposed to dividing subjects into highly specialized subfields. In addition to our classroom work, we ran laps in the municipal park every morning and did an hour of gymnastics.

I received my high school diploma from the Lichtwark School in 1928. One of the subjects in which I chose to be examined was socialism as it related to the nationalities question. I prepared myself by reading a lot of Adler and other Austrian Marxists. I supplemented their ideas with my own, or what I took to be my own. As I follow events in Central and Eastern Europe today, I regret that I no longer have in my possession the exam I wrote in 1928.

Since the Lichtwark School was experimental, the officials

who administered our final examinations were unusually strict. Nevertheless, nobody in my class failed.

Every class arranged its own graduation celebration. We put on Gogol's *Inspector General* for the next class, and they in turn gave us a party. Everybody made their own costume out of batiks.

The school staged a number of plays from 1921 to 1932, ranging from Kleist's *Der zerbrochene Krug* (The broken jug) to Brecht's *Der Jasager und der Neinsager* (He who says yes and he who says no). Brecht was a young dramatist then, and we devoured everything he wrote. Karl Kraus came up from Vienna especially for us. Even the Catholic philosopher Romano Guardini came to visit us at the school's invitation.

When you look at old photographs, you get an idea of the fashions of the day. I wore my hair in long braids. Linsey-woolsey dresses inspired by the Youth Movement* were much in style. Women and girls still didn't wear pants. Rather, they wore *rubashkas,* Russian-style blouses with a collar that buttoned on the side.

We took many group trips. When we studied life in the Middle Ages, for instance, we took excursions to Bad Wimpfe on the Neckar River and to Nuremberg. Another year we went to Holland, crisscrossing the country on bicycle. We were one of the first classes to visit England after World War I; I remember nearly every day of that trip. In London, for example, we lived in large assembly halls and met with members of the No More War Movement, a pacifist youth organization sponsored by the Quakers. Given the conditions that existed in schools at that time, just the number of trips we took made us unique. Other schools were precluded from

---

*The Youth Movement (Jugendbewegung) burgeoned after 1900 and consisted of an elite group of young people from the "new middle class" and also from the working class. Their main purpose was to organize independently their leisure activities. In the 1920s their lifestyles became more modern. Alongside campfire romanticism there arose a willingess to practice "socialism" in work camps. — Trans.

offering these kinds of opportunities because of their rigid time schedules. We became acquainted firsthand with different languages, cultures, and histories not as dry academic subjects but through direct exposure [to other countries].

Solidarity and mutual assistance were the hallmarks of our relationships with one another.

I was practically in love with my teacher Rudolf Kappe. He was highly educated and spoke excellent English. He was also a socialist and studied Karl Marx, Freud, and the Bible with us.

I still vividly remember one particular episode. The boys got hold of a large sheet of canvas, a kind of springboard. I sat in the middle of the sheet, my knees tucked into my chest, and was tossed several yards into the air. I could see my teacher while I was in motion. He had shut his eyes in horror, probably thinking that I wasn't going to land on the open canvas. Everything turned out all right, though. I suppose this episode epitomizes my life.

Later, while attending university I visited Kappe together with my friend Werner Bockelmann. Kappe and I stayed on such good terms with each other that I would bring my boyfriends to meet him and then get him to appraise them. Kappe was killed in action during the Second World War somewhere in Romania.

Incidentally, some years after I graduated, former chancellor Helmut Schmidt became a student at the Lichtwark School. He is just as enthusiastic about his experience there as I am, though we had different teachers, of course.

The school was Nazified in 1933, that is, in effect it ceased to exist. Sadly, despite a number of initiatives launched after 1945, it never reopened.

❖

Member of the KPD

My first encounter with the Communist Party took place on May 1, 1928. I boarded a streetcar near my house and rode alone to the big May Day celebration on the Moorweide in Hamburg to watch people demonstrate. Even though I didn't know a soul among the multitudes streaming onto the heath and felt very much alone, I believed I was doing the right thing. I can't really say I had a warm feeling. If anything, I felt like an outsider. I wondered what would it would be like to join the party without knowing a single member. Still, I felt as though I had to take the leap. I had just turned nineteen.

There was a boy named Harald Müller who was half a year behind me in school. I knew he was a member of the Communist youth movement and tried for some time to engage him in conversation, since I felt that what I was doing at the time—reading, discussing, and theorizing in a vacuum about philosophy—was utterly meaningless. I felt that the Communist Party was where I belonged but had no idea how to go about joining. So I finally asked him. He immediately presented me with a book entitled *What the Young Communist Should Know*. Then he proudly walked me down to Valentinskamp, the headquarters of the Communist Party in Hamburg, and introduced me to the local officials. I didn't know anybody there, but I was convinced that I was doing the right thing. Perhaps my move wasn't too well thought out. In any event, I can no longer recall precisely the reasons that prompted me to take the step. I simply believed that the Communists were the only ones who would champion the cause of justice and could change the world. As difficult as it may be to understand today, it should not be forgotten that this was a time when people from all segments of society—often the most courageous and morally resolute—were attracted to the party. I had of course read Karl Marx, and the spirit of the Lichtwark School played a part, too.

At any rate, Harald Müller beamed when I signed the membership application. People at headquarters urged me to enter the Communist youth movement, but I told them that I wanted to enter the party directly.

Though my new comrades no doubt regarded me as an oddity, they nevertheless accepted me. There was a large library at party headquarters on Valentinskamp, and I often browsed the collection during my first semester at university.

Romantic attachments also played a part, of course. The first "man" in my life was Ernst Noffke, head of the Kommunistische Studentenfraktion (Communist Student Faction), or the Kostufra, in Hamburg. He was a true friend. He apparently fell for me right after we met in the Kostufra. Though I wasn't in love with him, I felt it was high time for me to sleep with a man, and so I went to bed with him during one of our outings. I found the experience a bit odd and felt estranged from myself. Noffke came from a lower-middle-class family of teachers. His father was no longer alive, and he had a brother who later fled to Sweden. He himself ended up in the Soviet Union. I never learned the exact circumstances of his life in Russia, since I didn't stay in touch with him. He eventually found a wife there and fathered a girl named Ruth. From our time in Hamburg I knew that he had written a paper critical of the party, though I never actually saw it. From the beginning I, too, had certain misgivings about party policy and tried to find someone to support my position. However, he never showed me what he had written, perhaps out of deference to party discipline. I expect he ended up destroying the paper. His criticisms probably led to his undoing, for he was placed under arrest in the Soviet Union in 1937 and sent to a [labor] camp.

I became a member of a university cell, but because of my strict moral principles, I felt that as a Communist I shouldn't spend all my time with students; I had to get to know workers as well.

Immediately after graduating from high school in Harburg, I got a job in a factory for three months as a textile worker. I wanted to live like a worker in order to have a better understanding of what I was talking about when the subject of the working class came up during cell meetings and indoctrination sessions. My family was in quite an uproar because they thought I was going to starve to death on the income I received from the factory. However, I refused to take any handouts from home and wanted to live on my earnings alone. This was a matter of great importance to me. My girlfriend Ruth Tassoni witnessed what I was going through at the time and called me "little Saint Joan of the stockyards."

I was well received by my new comrades, and my life was quite bearable. I still remember a fellow party member in Harburg telling me, "I'll protect you with these hands, so you have no reason to be afraid." He had a Polish name and was a giant of a man with enormous hands. When you placed yours in his, it was like putting them to bed.

As party practice called for, I proceeded to build a cell within the textile factory and put out a little newsletter, until those who had helped to get me the job began—and rightly so—to view my activities as an attempt to circumvent their authority. Here comes this little bourgeoise and starts to agitate and cause trouble at work . . .

Nevertheless, I learned a great deal in the process, including some not-so-pleasant things. For example, in talking to women workers, I was repulsed by their vulgar jokes. Prior to my work in the factory, I had a different image of workers.

Though everybody in the factory knew that my background was different from theirs and considered me an oddball, they nevertheless accepted me. Once, our maid Mariechen brought me some chocolate from home, since she thought I was starving. Mariechen always spoiled me when I was a child. This time, however, I refused to accept her gift.

My aim was to learn how workers really lived. I wanted to know whether a person could survive on what a factory job paid. I realize that three months isn't long; however, no one wanted me to stay on the job longer than that, anyway. My political activities alone precluded the possibility of extending my tenure. In fact, the job turned out to be no more than a kind of practicum. I didn't recall causing much of a stir until Ruth Tassoni recently reminded me: "Don't you remember the brouhaha you caused when you worked at the factory?"

Members of the Communist Party were obliged to be part of a cell, be it in a factory or a residential district. I belonged to the Eimsbüttel district cell. I began as a regular member, but it wasn't long before I became an instructor at the Marxistische Arbeiterschule (Marxist Workers' School), or MASCH, where I developed a certain following. The MASCH was an evening school where politics and Marxist theory were discussed. I was deadly serious about my instructional work, because I was totally convinced that people could be changed according to the principles of Marxism.

Even though I've lost faith in dogmatic theories, I must admit that even now I believe that, in certain circumstances, you can change people. Clearly, this is difficult to do, but to this day I believe that people are eager to change themselves and the world.

In the MASCH I tried to present in simplified fashion what Marx had expressed in complicated terms. I based my lectures on the well-known MASCH publications by Duncker, Goldschmidt, and Wittfogel. The classes were attended mostly by male workers and their wives, including on one occasion one of my father's female patients, who later shocked my father when she told him about my activities.

I gradually rose within the ranks of the Communist Party, from being a member of a cell that comprised a single building to working as a functionary in Agitprop, that is, the Agitation and Propaganda Section. My work as a party agitator brought me into contact with literature, with the so-called "working-class writers" organized within the Bund proletarisch-revolutionärer Schriftsteller (Federation of Proletarian-Revolutionary Writers). My husband-to-be, Heinz Liepman, was a member of the federation, but I was barely aware of his existence at the time. Alfred Kurella (1895–1975), a popular Berlin writer, was also a member. Willi Bredel (1901–64), with whom I was well acquainted at the time, played an important role in the Hamburg branch of the federation. He was an intelligent man, but I never regarded him as a great writer; I knew, however, that he was a reliable party member. Bredel described me as follows: "Though she comes from a bourgeois household, she's one of us." I can still recall how proud I was when he expressed his faith in me. I even assisted in the staging of some Agitprop political plays.

As a political agitator I would be trucked into the countryside on Sundays along with fellow party members to try to persuade farmers not to pay their taxes and debts. Our work was part of the famous Landvolk-Bewegung (Country Folk Movement) in Schleswig-Holstein described by Hans Fallada in his novel *Bauern, Bonzen und Bomben* (Farmers, bigwigs, and bombs, 1931).* Among the Dithmarschen farmers I met individuals from a number of different groups, including the onetime leaders of the farmers' movment, Bruno von Salomon and Bodo Uhse (1904–63), both of whom had moved from the far Right to the extreme Left (the KPD) during this period. Bruno's brother, the writer Ernst von Salomon (1902–72), originally of a nationalist posture, was also a member of the agrarian movement.

Quite a few people from the nationalist camp found a second home in the Communist Party in those days. I spent a great deal of time talking with them about the so-called national question, which they invariably considered the starting point for any discussion. In Hamburg we met in taverns and homes. My place was something of a haven for many people, and I would spend whole nights passionately discussing issues during party meetings and at university. At first my

---

*Hans Fallada, *Bauern, Bonzen und Bomben* (Berlin: E. Rowohlt, 1931).

assignment was to establish contact with Bruno von Salomon and Bodo Uhse and familiarize them with the work of the Communist Party. In this I was successful, though they were already in the process of informing themselves. All members of the group were on close terms with one another. I liked to accompany them on their Sunday forays into the countryside surrounding Hamburg, calling on the farmers to rebel. Bodo and Bruno had a thorough understanding of the farmer mentality, and I learned a great deal from both of them. Together with Ernst von Salomon, they published newspapers for farmers in which they explained the cause of the agrarian crisis and incited them to civil disobedience. All three men were well-known journalists and writers. Bruno von Salomon was much closer to the party than Ernst, who still had some reservations. Incidentally, Ernst described this colorful period in great detail in his autobiography *Der Fragebogen* (1951).[*] Ernst remained in Germany during the entire Nazi period. Bruno became an ardent Communist and was active in the underground during the Third Reich. After Hitler came to power, Ernst once saved me from being sent to prison when the police were about to arrest me during a roundup. "Not this one, " he said, "she's a good friend of mine." To many people Ernst von Salomon was a national hero because of his involvement in the murder of Walter Rathenau, a crime for which he was sentenced to five years in prison.

While living as an émigré in Amsterdam, I would occasionally visit Bruno von Salomon and Bodo Uhse in Paris. Bodo's girlfriend, Ellen Gottschalk, was the daughter of an American diplomat. Before returning to the States, she told me to "take care of Bodo, he obviously loves you," which was indeed the case. Though I liked him very much, I wanted our relationship to have no strings attached. I never enoyed reading his

---

[*]Ernst von Salomon, *Der Fragebogen* (Hamburg: Rowohlt, 1951); English trans. by Constantine Fitzgibbon: *The Answers of Ernst von Salomon to the 131 Questions in the Allied Military Government "Fragebogen"* (London: Putnam, 1954), and *Fragebogen: The Questionnaire* (Garden City, N.Y.: Doubleday, 1954).

books, yet he always wanted me to praise his poems. I found them dreadful, though. They were filled with men on horseback, and I always had to laugh when he read them to us or gave them to us as gifts. Riding, riding, riding—it sounded a little like Rilke in *Die Weise von Liebe und Tod des Cornets Christoph Rilke* (The lay of the love and death of Cornet Christoph Rilke)—or like an epigone of Rilke. Bruno's brother Ernst von Salomon had published books even before 1933; he remained in Germany and for a time became a reader at the Rowohlt publishing house.

In Paris Bruno and Bodo took me to every part of the city—the marketplaces, bars, and restaurants. They both did a lot of writing for newspapers and had decent accomodations. I met a number of artists and writers through them and got the impression that they were not unhappy living in exile.

After the war Bruno visited me and my future husband Heinz Liepman in Hamburg. He was suffering from tuberculosis and died soon afterward. Bodo Uhse became a well-known party writer and an official in the German Democratic Republic. I once visited him in East Berlin. His home was in an enclosed area where a number of other artists and writers lived. He had a car and a chauffeur at his disposal. I found this somewhat excessive, but he was oblivious to my criticisms. He was the perfect apparatchik and stopped short of discussing anything that concerned the party, believing that whatever he said could be misinterpreted. While he was living as a refugee in France, on the other hand, he was always pleasant and good-humored. He had a wonderful laugh—a real belly laugh—and a pleasant voice. As with so many other former rightists, his past haunted him to the end. Time and again he had to justify the fact that he had switched sides.

The Communist Party was rife with internecine conflicts. I found it particularly painful that the various factions tried to take advantage of me for their own purposes when disputes arose. I was too naive and didn't realize what was happening; I just sensed that something was going on. This was one of the main reasons that I developed a certain emotional resistance to the various currents within the party: the right wing and the right of center, the appeasers, the Trotskyists, the left deviationists, and Lord knows what else—every imaginable kind of deviationist. I was completely disoriented and realized that the idealistic image I had of the Communists was very different from the reality. Intrigue was rampant, and my naïveté was easily exploited. However, they never really succeeded in using me for their own ends. I was clearly too strong-willed for most of them. For instance, they constantly sought to condemn "appeasers," whereas I always thought the various currents within the party should be reconciled and that it was wrong to exaggerate differences. The party leaders, however, believed in the strict separation of party factions and the need to combat "appeasers." Consequently, I tried more and more to dissociate myself from the day-to-day operations of the party. Toward the end of the Weimar Republic, for instance, I felt that Communists and Social Democrats should join in proclaiming a general strike in opposition to the Fascists. The party leaders, however, believed that the Social Democrats were as much or more of a threat than the Fascists, precisely because they were our brothers, that is, the enemy within. Nevertheless, there were many who felt as I did.

During my second semester in Berlin, I was nearly drawn into these intrigues in spite of myself. Through Ernst Noffke I met the party functionary Hans Kippenberger, whom I mentioned earlier. Ernst had the greatest respect for Hans, and from time to time I would see him in Berlin, where he tried to talk me into working for the party apparat. The leaders of the party had set up a clandestine military apparatus or organization within the party—the so-called M Apparat—to keep an eye on the various factions. Hans obviously thought I was sufficiently untainted and inconspicuous to carry out undercover operations. I turned him down when I realized what he had in mind. Quite naively I had expected the Communist Party to be unified, without one group spying on the other.

Legal Studies in Hamburg and Berlin

Though I often fought with my parents when I was young, our relationship was basically sound. My mother was a housewife, and although she had a maid and a cleaning lady, she still had the primary responsibility for raising two small children. She wasn't a "social" person. Rather, she was frank and direct. She was clearly more adept at dealing with day-to-day chores than was my father, who was a dedicated doctor. His patients kept him busy night and day, and he suffered when he was unable to help them. He was a dreamer and loved nature. It was from him that I inherited my reverence for all living things.

Politically, he was close to the German Democratic Party (Deutsche Demokratische Partei, or DDP). However, he never became a member because he was too involved in the work of his profession. Though he discussed politics a lot, he didn't do much more than talk. He was a voracious reader. Even when I was a little girl, he would take me by the hand every Saturday and walk to the shop of a Hamburg bookseller named Gold-schmidt-Glogau. He bought both medical books and belles lettres. For years I thought that buying books was what Saturdays were for.

He was a very popular doctor in Hamburg and had a large practice. Later, when it became known that I was an active member of the Communist Party, he got into quite a bit of trouble. A rumor spread that I had marched at the head of a parade and carried a flag. It was untrue, of course, but there were many such rumors, which is why my father was one of the first doctors in Hamburg forbidden by the Nazis to participate in the national health-care program or treat welfare patients. He was extremely unhappy, of course, because he lived for his work. This put quite a strain on me, even though my parents never actually blamed me [for the problems I caused them].

The first and last time I was ever slapped was while I was attending university—my father was the perpetrator. I was in love, and my boyfriend, Werner Bockelmann, brought me home late one evening. Although my parents had already gone to bed, they were still awake. I knew where the stairs creaked and which steps to avoid in order not to be noticed, but my efforts were to no avail. My father came downstairs. "Where were you?" he snapped. "Werner and I were outside smooching," I replied. He was so upset he slapped me in the face.

He at once regretted what he had done and wasn't able to sleep a wink that night. I, for my part, unabashedly exploited his lack of restraint. "Please accept my formal apology," he said the next morning. I played the injured party: "I'm not going to stay in a house in which I've been slapped."

After that I moved out and rented a room—which my parents paid for. I wasn't earning anything, after all; I was going to school. I ended up living near the university in a room in a spanking new building where I had kitchen and bathroom privileges—a typical student abode. I subsequently reconciled with my parents, but I no longer wanted to live at home. After all, I was a grown-up.

I spent my first semester in Hamburg and my second in Berlin, since I enjoyed the cultural life in the capital. One of the first reviews I ever wrote—of Brecht's and Weills's *Aufstieg und Fall der Stadt Mahagonny* (The rise and fall of the city of Mahagonny)—was published in the *Kommunistische Volkszeitung*. I lived in a room in the Wedding section of Berlin. I had traveled from Hamburg to Berlin with a few friends, including Johanna Zorn, whom I had known both at the Lichtwark School and through the KPD. It was mainly her idea that we share a flat. She died after the war in the GDR, where she worked for the State Planning Commission. Before the war she and I, together with her brother, were members of the Kostufra. Her brother, Max, later became a mathematics professor and emigrated to America.

I had contacts within the Berlin KPD before I actually arrived after my first semester of university. I was on good terms with Richard Löwenthal, for example, who was a member of the Young Communists at the time. He never had much money, whereas I received a decent allowance from my parents, so I often invited him over for a bite. When I told him about Kippenberger's suggestion that I become a member of the KPD's security apparatus, he was totally nonplussed: "My God, how could he possibly consider you for something like that. Talk about being miscast!" How right he was!

It was common in those days to move several times from one university to another. Moreover, the faculty at Berlin University included such outstanding scholars as Professor Wolf in property law and other important figures in the fields of law, philosophy, and economics.

My choice of profession was indirectly connected to my father. My high school diploma indicated that I would go on to study medicine. That had always been my father's dream; one day he actually told me how much he was looking forward to sharing a practice with me. The idea that I would be tied to my father's practice for the rest of my life so horrified me that I did everything I could to preclude the possibility. At the same time, I didn't want to hurt him. Since this was such an important matter to him, I had to think up an acceptable alternative in order to extricate myself from this predicament. So I told him I would prefer to study law. After I began my legal studies, I found that I actually enjoyed the field of law; it was a subject that interested and stimulated me. I planned to go on and work as an assistant to Professor Rudolf von Laun, an instructor of mine who taught public law at Hamburg University. Political events, however, precluded that possibility.

Though I wasn't the only female law student in those days,

there were still only a small number of women studying law; however, I never felt discriminated against. My female political comrades-in-arms urged me to become involved in the women's movement. I declined to do so, though, because I believed that the women's question was basically a men's question as well.

During my first few semesters I was primarily interested in the philosophy of law and then in the introductory courses on civil and criminal law. At the time I had no idea, of course, how useful my legal education would ultimately be to my career as a literary agent twenty-five years later. Because I was politically committed, my original plan was to become a judge of the juvenile court. All my plans came to naught, though, as a result of political developments. Later, when I was a refugee in Holland and worked in a law office, circumstances led me to continue my education in The Hague and develop a specialty in conflict of laws.

I passed the first state examination in good time, after three and a half years at university. It was a lengthy examination during which we were tested in different subject competencies. In 1933 I undertook my first attempt to prepare for the second state examination in order to attain the grade of "Assessor." I began to undergo preliminary in-service training: six weeks on the registration and transfer of land titles; two months on criminal law, on courts that had jurisdiction over guardians and wards, the public prosecutor's office, etcetera. However I was never allowed to take the examination.

To get the doctorate in spite of the obstacles that had been thrown in my path, I contrived to have Professor von Laun supervise my dissertation, which dealt with a boring but manageable subject. A dispute had arisen in Austria regarding an employee of a foreign mission who claimed diplomatic immunity. Using the latest material from the case, I wrote about the problem of diplomatic immunity as it affected the employees of foreign missions in general, a subject that had been discussed myriad times before.

My in-service training for the second state examination in law was immediately terminated in 1933. I was among the first to be prohibited from pursuing a chosen profession. Incidentally, I believe that I was initially prevented from taking the exam because I was a Communist and not because I was a Jew. When Hitler became chancellor in 1933, I, as opposed to most other Communists, felt that the Nazi phenomenon wasn't going to disappear overnight—I felt it would last between one and two years.

A number of my friends tried to leave Germany as quickly as possible. At first it was relatively easy to do so. Later, the various host countries made this avenue of escape more difficult. Almost all my friends in the Hamburg branch of the KPD were arrested, and many subsequently perished as a result. Those who weren't caught, however, continued to meet—clandestinely, of course. Little by little we adapted to the changed circumstances and became correspondingly cautious. For instance, only two or three people would ever meet at one time.

I once heard Hitler speak at a Nazi rally. For me the worst part of this experience was his hysterical outbursts. It was horrible to see the way in which the audience responded in hysterical fashion to a hysteric. I was shocked at how he was able to sway them with nothing but lies. He captivated the audience with catchphrases such as "revenge for Versailles." His mendacity was disgusting. Ever since, I've been sensitive to extreme nationalism, particularly when espoused by Germans.

I recently saw an example of this kind of attitude when I was visiting Florence. A group of five or six Germans, all of them drunk, were acting as though the whole Piazza Signoria belonged to them—and they did so quite brazenly, as if it were their perfect right. The sentiments that give rise to chauvinism and were exploited by Hitler continue to exist. Of course, there are also positive national sentiments, for example, the love of one's native language, a feeling that I share. Perhaps my inability to understand national sentiments is a function of my life. I am German-born, but I am also a Jew and a Swiss. Yet I tend to think of Holland as my home, since that is where I spent the most important part of my life.

In spite of violence in the streets and the Reichstag fire, the Nazis captured just 44 percent of the votes cast in the last even semilegitimate election of March 5, 1933—and even this figure was obviously fabricated. My father asked a policeman who was walking up and down the street in front of our house and whom we knew quite well, "Do you think this was a fair election?" "Listen, *Herr Doktor,* it's still all right to ask *me* that question, but, whatever you do, don't ask anyone else. Pretty soon you won't be able to get any answer to a question like that—just asking it could land you in prison."

The morning after the Reichstag fire, I was sitting in a comrade's flat in Berlin. All of a sudden Ernst von Salomon burst into the room, grabbed me by the hand, and said, "You're coming with me to Hamburg. I'm getting you on the first train out of Berlin. The situation here is too unpredictable." The day before the fire, February 26, 1933, I had been in the Communist Party's chambers in the Reichstag, a fact that was widely known. And it was feared that I might have left traces of my presence there. I had sat on a window ledge and met with Karl Olbrysch (1902–40), a Communist Reichstag deputy. My situation was becoming increasingly precarious; however, I believed that the political decision as to who would control Germany was still pending. The storm troopers were on parade everywhere, but so were the Communists. We still felt that the two sides would come to blows and that we would emerge victorious. Besides the main Communist paramilitary organization Roter Frontkämpferbund (Red Frontline Fighters' League), or RFB, there was also the Rote Marine (Red Navy, an auxiliary combat group of the RFB), whose members, incidentally, violated their oath and promptly deserted to the Nazis.

❖

Werner Bockelmann

I met Werner Bockelmann at university while I was taking one of the customary cram courses in law. He was seated next to me, and I was immediately attracted to him. It was love at first sight. In fact, we both knew the first day we met that we were meant for each other. And for quite some time we never doubted that we would be together forever. He was bright, charming, and a marvelous flirt. I was also attracted by the fact that he was a conservative, had grown up on a farm, and lived in Barendorf. I felt straightaway that we had to have a serious discussion about politics and that I might be able to change his opinions. I was motivated, among other things, by the desire to change another human being. For our first rendezvous we had to cancel dates with other people, and both of us felt terribly guilty. I remember our first evening together. We went dancing, and because I was so short and he was so tall, he nibbled playfully at my long braids. The ploy worked; I thought he was funny and imaginative, different from the others. The fact that he came from another world was an added attraction, particularly since he was so proud of his family and background. His father had been a banker in Moscow until 1917; his mother was Russian. The family had escaped to Sweden during the Revolution. The eldest son, Erwin, was the director of a large oil refinery in Hamburg. Then there was Rudi, who managed a farm in Carinthia, in Austria; Gerd, also a farmer; and Johnny, the youngest, a lawyer now living in Frankfurt. We used to run into one another at the Frankfurt book fair.

Werner was astute, quick-witted, cultured, well read, and a

fine lawyer. His sons Andrej, Martin, and Thomas inherited his charm. Thomas is the sucessful artistic director of the arena stage in Tübingen. Andrej has been working for a number of years as a freelance television journalist, mainly for Hessian Radio in Frankfurt.

Werner and I used to spend whole evenings together arguing about Marxist philosophy and the theory of surplus value, subjects that were of great importance to me at the time. I recall that he nearly bopped me once when I said, "Those swinish farmers don't appropriate their surplus value directly, but don't worry, they get their profit, by fair means or foul."

Werner was two years older than I. He'd taken, among other things, some engineering courses, initially with the intention of becoming an engineer. He was a semester behind me in taking the state examination in law.

I considered our relationship all-encompassing; we did everything together: studied, read, flirted, slept, and nearly beat each other up—as I said, we did everything. Before taking me to visit his home in Barendorf for the first time, Werner asked me whether I ate squab. I said yes. He was surprised and relieved. His father nevertheless refused to meet me; he always disappeared whenever I showed up. Werner quarreled a lot with his brothers because of me. He even came to blows with his eldest brother on my account. What sparked the altercation was when his brother said he wouldn't sleep in the same bed in which Werner had gone to bed with a Jew. The Nazi dictatorship was already casting its shadow . . . My visits to Barendorf were always somewhat of an ordeal, but one from which I intended to emerge triumphant.

The upshot of our endless political discussions was that Werner applied for membership in the Communist Party.

There was a problem during the first few weeks of our relationship—another man, namely, the Communist Karl Olbrysch. All of us—Karl, Werner, and I—suffered greatly at the time. However, I was quite sure of what I wanted and decided quickly in favor of Werner.

It was impossible for me to imagine that Werner could be

any less certain, in spite of an incident that I didn't recall until long afterward. Shortly after we met, we were sauntering down Schlüterstrasse in Hamburg, when a girl came walking toward us from the other side of the street. Werner turned to me and said, "Wait a moment. I have a little something to take care of." When he returned, he informed me that she was a former girlfriend of his who had come to Hamburg to study because of him. "What did you say?" I asked. "I told her it was all over," he replied.

The incident is as fresh in my mind today as when it happened. How strange, I thought, you can't just end a relationship like that in the middle of the street. Since I had just fallen in love, I repressed the memory. I never dreamed that the same thing could happen to me . . .

Karl Olbrysch moved from Hamburg to Berlin, where he became a Communist Reichstag deputy. He was seized during the mass arrests that followed the Reichstag fire. One day Werner phoned me: "It says in the paper that Karl has been arrested. I'll be right over." Karl Olbrysch spent some time in prison before his release was secured. The last stage in the effort to save him ended in tragedy when the ship that was supposed to take him and his girlfriend to begin a new life in America or New Zealand sank.

Though I didn't panic when Werner phoned to tell me about Karl Olbrysch's arrest, I realized that my situation had become extremely serious. I also knew that Karl wouldn't reveal anything about me if he were interrogated.

Conditions in Germany had become intolerable. People were being arrested and murdered everywhere. I realized that I was in great danger, even though a warrant for my arrest wasn't issued until after I was already in Holland. I have no idea why I escaped arrest in Germany. Houses were being searched everywhere, my family's included,[*] which is why I

---

[*]Digest of the investigation files of the Hamburg police and court authority, 1933.

no longer have any letters or photos from the time before
1933. As noted earlier, my father was one of the first physicians in Hamburg prohibited from participating in the national health-care program or treating welfare patients, the reason
being that I was considered a political threat.

My parents stood by me and defended me—at least to
other people—in spite of the dreadful consequences. When
there was any blame to pass around, it was done within the
family circle: "Why did you do such and such? Maybe Daddy
wouldn't have had to endure all this if you had just quit the
Communist Party." I found myself in a difficult situation. In
April 1934 I escaped arrest by fleeing to Holland.

❊

Exile in Holland

I left Germany for Amsterdam on April 22, 1934, my twen-
ty-fifth birthday. Why Amsterdam? It was the émigré center closest to Hamburg. I was absolutely convinced that the
Germans would overthrow the Nazis and liberate themselves
from Hitler in the not-too-distant future. I didn't want to be
too far from the revolution or my hometown.

Werner Bockelmann and Fritz Einstein, a Hamburg physician and close friend, took me to the station. Along with my
two suitcases, I carried a large wicker bottle filled with ink. I
had no idea what kind of work I would do in Holland or what
I would have to live on. From my parents in Germany I was
to receive a remittance of ten marks a month, the maximum
allowed by law. While I was still in Hamburg, a woman talked
me into buying the bottle of ink. "I have something here," she
insisted, "that'll provide you with an income when you get to
Holland." There were a number of banks and a lot of wealthy
people in Holland, she said. Consequently, a large number of
checks were being drawn, attracting a concomitant number of
con artists and check forgers. "I've developed a chemical agent
to make truly indelible ink. All other inks can be washed
away, but not this one." She showed me how to demonstrate
the use of her miracle ink, and I really believed that I would
have a job as soon as I crossed the Dutch border.

When I arrived, though, I didn't even make an attempt to go
to a bank and say, "How do you do? You know, there are a lot
of con artists here, and I'm sure this indelible ink I'm selling is
just what you need." I was nearly at my wit's end, when I realized how ridiculous the whole idea was, in fact. What was I to

do in a country where I didn't understand the language and barely knew a living soul?

My first contact in Amsterdam was a doctor who had once taken charge of my father's practice when my father went on vacation. I looked him up on my first day in Holland; he allowed me to stay with him and his family for a week.

More often than not, it was sheer good fortune that accounted for the friends and acquaintances I made in Holland over the next few years. I had many letters of reference, but I didn't feel comfortable using them. They came from the bank of M. M. Warburg & Co. in Hamburg. One of the proprietor's daughters, Ingrid, was a friend of mine and had advised me not to go to Holland without references: "At least let my father give you a few letters to take with you."

I knew a Jewish girl in Holland whom I'd met on a ski trip, so I phoned her after I arrived. She told me how happy she was that I was in town, because she had a job interview that very day. She was a handweaver and knew the owner of a weaving mill. She invited me to accompany her to the interview, since she wasn't sure whether she would take a job at the mill. So both of us went there together. Suddenly the owner turned to me and asked, "What do you do for a living?" "Nothing," I replied, "I just came here from Hamburg." Then he looked at my hands and said, "We manufacture handwoven cloth and carpets here. You can work with me, and I'll teach you the art of the loom. I can tell that you have the hands of a weaver." Since this was my first chance to work, I readily accepted the offer. The first week on the job I earned 7.50 guilders, that is, virtually nothing. Later, my salary was raised to 10 guilders a week—a little more, but still not enough to live on. I paid 7.50 guilders a week just for a tiny furnished room on Rijnstraat in the inner part of southern Amsterdam. The people there were quite nice, and a number of other émigrés lived there as well.

A short time later the mill closed. Was it because the owner had raised my salary to 10 guilders a week? All kidding aside, he actually had some very good ideas. He came from Ticino and had invented a loom that resembled the heavy wooden looms of the past but was made of light aluminum. Part of it had to be operated by hand and part of it worked mechanically. I learned a great deal about weaving and fabrics and had a lot of fun to boot. At the end of the day I could say with some pride that I had produced two yards of cloth or carpet. I felt good about having created something that people could actually hold in their hands. We worked in a large building that had once been part of a factory, and we were given quite a bit of autonomy. I used to imagine that someday when I was old and had the time, I could weave for as long as my heart desired. I loved the peaceful nature of the work and the fact that I could both meditate and produce something tangible at the same time.

Thank goodness I always had an opportunity to have lunch at a friend's place, a circumstance that was connected to the one time I actually used a letter of reference. The letter was addressed to a certain Herr Felix Tikotin. "This gentleman is quite a bit older than you," the Warburgs had told me, "but you'll like him nevertheless." After taking the job as a weaver, I overcame my initial shyness and set off to find apartment 707 on the corner of Leidsestraat and Prinsengracht. It was a rather hot day in early May. A fantastically beautiful long-legged girl walked ahead of me as I climbed the stairs. I rang the doorbell, but nobody answered. So I decided to walk up to the next floor. At the top of the stairs I came upon a roof garden, where a portly man was seated stark naked. He draped a towel around his waist and asked me who I was. "Ruth Lilienstein," I replied. "I'm from Hamburg. This is my first time in Holland. Please accept this letter of reference from the Warburgs; it's addressed to you." He asked me to wait. Then he went downstairs, got dressed, and came back up to that delightful roof garden in the heart of the city. In the meantime he had read the letter, the contents of which were quite flattering. We then talked, and he showed me his lovely Japanese drawings and prints. At one time he had lived in Berlin and Dresden. He was an architect by profession and had spent a lifetime collecting Japanese art, on which he was an expert. He was an art dealer as well as an ardent collector. I was immediately smitten, but not by him—by his prints and drawings. Among other things, he had organized the Warburgs' *netsuke* collection. *Netsuke* are miniature works of art—carvings in wood and ivory—which served as toggles for the pouches that Japanese men hung from the obi of their pocketless kimonos.

Finally he asked me what I did for a living. I told him about my job at the weaving mill, after which we discussed a variety of other topics: *The Thousand and One Nights;* the Warburgs and Hamburg; Hitler; and my personal plans. As we parted, he invited me to have lunch with him on a regular basis. "I do my own cooking," he said, "and I'm quite good at it. You have to eat at least one warm meal a day or you'll drop." I accepted his invitation, and from then on I had lunch in his apartment every day at noon. I met a number of people through him, especially people interested in Japanese and other Asian art.

The following anecdote illustrates how people helped one another in those days. Despite the fact that Tikotin didn't really know me, he nonetheless lent me 1,000 guilders, the amount needed to obtain Dutch residence and work permits. I deposited the 1,000 guilders in a bank account and received a transaction receipt, which I then took to the immigration authorities in order to obtain the proper permits. A month later I closed the account and returned the money to Tikotin. Incidentally, the account then contained only 999.75 guilders, since the bank had charged 25 cents to carry the account!

This story also demonstrates just how helpful Dutch officials were at the time, for it was the Dutch immigration authorities themselves who showed me exactly how to deposit money in an account for a limited time in order to "document" the fact that I had sufficient savings to support myself without working . . . Now I was able to move about freely.

I remained friends with Tikotin, my first Dutch benefactor, until his death. He died about seven years ago in Vevey, Switzerland. To the very end, even when he was a frail old man, he had a vivid remembrance of those days in Holland.

He met his wife through me, which is one of the reasons we continued to remain on such close terms. It was only because of the warm meals he served me every day that I was able to endure the work at the weaving mill.

From the very beginning of my stay in Holland, I made every effort to learn Dutch, although I didn't make much progress at first. I had no formal instruction in the language; I just talked and talked and made a lot of mistakes. I didn't really learn to speak proper Dutch until I went underground and lived with a Dutch family. Being a foreigner, I had to learn how to keep a low profile, and my adopted family proved to be an excellent school in this regard.

Many of the émigrés were friendly with each other; they would invite one another to their homes and have get-togethers. Hans Kramer, a fellow student from Hamburg, married — of all people — a woman I had known in Hamburg. Through them I was introduced to the Oetingers, who lived two doors down. Fritz Oetinger had been one of the youngest prosecuting attorneys in Hamburg; he was a dedicated and talented lawyer. He and his wife were my best friends in Holland. Fritz was the scion of an old-line Hamburg family that had long been in the tobacco business. Since Fritz's German legal education didn't qualify him to practice law in Holland, he renewed his association with the tobacco industry after he immigrated to the Netherlands. The Oetingers were people of means, well bred, and had a flair for fashion.

After the Oetingers, my next best friend in Holland was Magda. She and her family had fled to Holland from Prague in 1939. Like me, she was a Communist and a Jew. Her father, Professor Starkenstein, a pharmacologist at Charles University in Prague, was forced to leave the city when the Germans occupied Czechoslovakia; he was later murdered by the Gestapo in Mauthausen concentration camp. Magda's brother was arrested the same day the Germans invaded Prague and was killed in a concentration camp after working for some time as a physician in Poland. We were unable to obtain any more information about his fate even after the war. Only Magda and her mother survived. Magda studied art history, was politically active, and was therefore in some danger. The threat to her safety, as well as to mine, derived not so much from the fact that she was Jewish as from the political nature of her activities. In 1941 she married Coen van Emde Boas, a very erudite psychiatrist and sexologist. He had, for example, translated Shakespeare's sonnets into Dutch. I would frequently spend time with them in their home before I was forced to go into hiding. We have remained good friends to this day. Magda works as an interpreter at conferences—she speaks six languages—and still lives in Amsterdam.

Sometimes we émigrés would simply get to know each other on the street and strike up a conversation. I made the acquaintance of one of my best girlfriends, Lisbeth Östreicher, on a streetcar. She was a weaver and knitter, had studied at the Bauhaus, and came from Karlsbad. Some members of her family had been living in Holland for quite some time already. In 1938 she arranged to have her sister, a student of photography at the Graphische Hochschule (Academy of Graphic Arts) in Vienna, join her in Holland. She then worked as a photographer under the name Maria Austria.

The émigrés weren't all in a depressed state of mind. Many of them were convinced that somehow or other Hitler would soon disappear from the scene. To my knowledge, the German émigrés didn't have a newspaper of their own at the time.

My experiences with the Dutch were uniformly positive. The Dutch whom I met were quite liberal and expressed delight whenever they met someone who had gotten out of Germany alive.

The Dutch tradition of freedom, a legacy of the victorious war of liberation against the Spanish, played a major part in shaping their attitudes. A number of my Dutch friends today don't see things in the same positive light that I do; however, when I came to Holland, everyone I met was helpful, open, and politically active.

After the weaving mill closed, I worked for some time as a secretary for German émigrés, including a stint for an attorney named John Rothschild, who together with another lawyer, Dr. Hugo Emmerich, wrote a study on the legal status of Germans in foreign countries, a book on which I collaborated (*Die Rechtslage deutscher Staatsangehöriger im Ausland* [The legal status of German citizens in foreign countries], 1937).* However, they couldn't acknowledge me as a coauthor, since the German police had issued a warrant for my arrest charging me with acts preparatory to the commission of high treason. They both felt they would have had to fear for their lives if my name had appeared on the book. That's how fearful people were of an imminent German invasion. Rothschild was later murdered by the Nazis in Westerbork, a police detention and transit camp for Jews in the Netherlands.

I also worked, of course, with the Communist émigrés, who, by the way, constituted a tiny minority of the refugees in Holland. Although there was comparatively more activity among the German Jewish émigrés, I was only marginally involved with them. The Museum of Jewish History in Amsterdam chronicles the impact of the German-Jewish émigrés on Dutch Jewry, not to mention Dutch culture generally. There were a great many writers, painters, and scientists among them, and their common bond—their homeland, as it were—was the German language. Since language means everything to a writer, writers suffered most as a result of being cut off from their roots, that is, the living language. Soon after 1933, however, a number of Dutch publishers established publishing houses in Amsterdam that specialized in the publication of works by German émigré writers in German. They included the firms of Allert de Lange, Querido, and van Kampen, to name just a few.

Certain strains developed between the political émigrés and members of the Jewish émigré community. The Jewish émigrés did not particularly want to get involved in politics, though they were all opposed to Hitler, of course. Many were mainly concerned with trying to get to America as quickly as

---

*Hugo Emmerich and John Rothschild, *Die Rechtslage deutscher Staatsangehöriger im Ausland* (Haarlem: H. D. Tjeenk Willink, 1937).

possible. Most of the clients of Dr. Rothschild's law firm were
Jews resident in Holland who were seeking to emigrate to
other countries. This was not a simple proposition given the
deadlines and local restrictions imposed wherever possible on
those wishing to enter another country. No sooner had someone obtained a visa for Mexico than the voyage itself became
problematic because of the time limits that were invariably
imposed on transit visas. The United States, for example, was
not admitting any more immigrants. Congress had set quotas
for each country [the Immigration Act of 1924], permitting
only a fixed number of Germans to enter the U.S. annually,
regardless of whether they were Jewish. The determining factor was national origin. Later, a so-called "Rescue Committee" was established to provide visas to additional numbers of
Jews and other victims of Nazi persecution who were in need
of special protection. There were also con artists, of course,
who preyed on people's fears, trying to make them believe
that they could help them escape from territories that were
exposed to danger. Unfortunately, many people were taken in
by these scams.

The Communist Party devised ways to smuggle people
into France and Portugal. On several occasions, in fact, I
passed on money from Jewish families to the KPD so that the
party could carry out just these kinds of relief missions. At the
time, the party needed the money in order to stay afloat.

Many refugees became extremely frightened as their situation grew more and more hopeless. I recall an incident that
began in the office of Dr. Rothschild's law firm. One of our
clients, a wealthy Belgian Jew, was in deep despair over the
ominous turn of events. After he left the office, I had a feeling
he was going to do something to himself, so I called him at his
hotel. He told me he was about to take his life. "Nowadays
it's impossible to live with a name like Karfunkelstein!" I
spent quite a bit of time talking with him and finally managed
to get him through the crisis. The next day he bought up every
rose in the flower shop on Leidesplein and had them sent to
me. However, I had no idea where to put them all. Since I had
only a tiny furnished room and was living a hand-to-mouth
existence, I considered selling them.

I later told the story of the roses to my husband Heinz Liepman, who used it in his novel *Karlchen, oder, die Tücken der Tugend* (Charlie, or the wiles of virtue, 1964).* In the book, though, he depicted me as throwing the roses out the window, which I hadn't done, of course. Actually, I gave them away. Since there weren't enough vases, I put a pail on every floor of the apartment house and distributed them throughout the building. I still remember asking myself why Karfunkelstein hadn't given me money instead. That would've been much more useful than roses. He invited me for lunch once after the episode with the roses. But after that I never heard from him again. Maybe it *was* impossible to live with a name like Karfunkelstein.

The Canadian writer Norman Levine wrote a different version of the episode and titled it "Django, Karfunkelstein, and Roses" in a collection of stories of the same name.†

All these events took place during the period before May 1940, that is, before the German invasion. In Germany, meanwhile, a warrant had been issued for my arrest charging me with undertaking acts preparatory to committing high treason. I was convicted in absentia. The warrant caused me particular distress because I feared for the people who knew me, for my family and friends. It also prevented me from being as actively involved politically as I wanted to be in Holland.

I traveled undercover from Holland to Germany several times during this period under orders from the Communist Party. Later, I also entered Germany via Switzerland. It was sheer folly, of course, but everything worked out well. I would carry sample flyers and information regarding future contacts and meeting places and then return with concealed parcels. I once had a clandestine meeting behind the choir of

---

*Heinz Liepman, *Karlchen, oder, die Tücken der Tugend* (Reinbek bei Hamburg: Rowohlt, 1964).

†Norman Levine, *Django, Karfunkelstein und Rosen* (Düsseldorf: Claasen, 1987); English original, "Django, Karfunkelstein, and Roses," *Encounter* 65 (December 1985): 3–6.

the Augsburg cathedral. I brought materials relevant to the survival of the party in Nazi Germany; however, I no longer remember exactly what they contained. We had to carry out these assignments as quickly as possible, which is part of the reason I can't recall the details today. The meeting, though, must have taken place before the beginning of the Spanish Civil War, because the agent who sent me to Augsburg, Hans Beimler (1895–1936), a leading Communist and commander in the Spanish Civil War, was later killed in Spain. He was living undercover in Switzerland under an assumed name and always walked with a dog at his side as a kind of front. He was an intelligent and very dedicated member of the party. Augsburg was his hometown, and his wife continued to live there. Since my meeting was in Augsburg, I took some things, mostly underwear, with me for his son, who was about twelve years old at the time. I fitted everything into my suitcase and on the way back exchanged the contents for contraband. The suitcase—which had a false bottom—popped open in transit, and it was all I could do to close it again. I was scared to death. On the train I put the suitcase between my legs and constantly fiddled with it, hoping all the time that nobody would notice me. Everything came off without a hitch, though. Hans Beimler met me at the station in Zurich and whisked me away. Since the train arrived late, he sweated blood thinking that something had gone wrong.

During an undercover visit to Berlin I once even ran into Werner Bockelmann. I had been sent there as a courier and stayed for a short time with Evchen Tikotin. Werner knew her, too, and happened to be in Berlin the same day I was in the city. He was shocked when he saw me, because he thought I was living out of harm's way in Amsterdam. Though it was extremely dangerous, he stayed with me. It was a wonderful and unexpected surprise.

In those days I loved and hated Germany at the same. I hated it because everything that meant anything to me had been destroyed. Relations between people had been utterly disrupted. I loved it because it was a stunningly beautiful country and German was my native language.

I was scared when carrying out these undercover missions. Although I was cautious, I was far from certain that I would survive. *Que será, será* was my motto. Maybe that's why I was an effective member of the underground. When others get flustered, I remain cool. Which is not to say that I'm a cold fish.

I would have liked to go to Spain, too, in 1936, but those in positions of authority within the party told me to stay put, that it was more important to continue doing what I was doing. My classmate Ruth Tassoni, née Domino, went to Spain via France, where she did service as a nurse. Many of the stories she published later take place against the backdrop of the Spanish Civil War.

That same year, 1936, I was invited to Moscow under the auspices of the Rote Hilfe (Red Relief). The Rote Hilfe was a subsidiary organiztion of the KPD. I ran into Hans Kippenberger on the streets of Moscow. He was living there in exile and was quite surprised to see me. He was eager to hear what conditions were like in Germany; however, I couldn't tell him much since I was living in Holland at the time. He resided in the Hotel Lux, where many prominent Communist émigrés were housed, including Walter Ulbricht and Herbert Wehner.

In those days I was unaware of the Stalinist excesses in the Soviet Union and dismissed negative information about Russia as enemy propaganda. During my discussions in Holland with the Communist attorney Bernd Karlsberg, I consistently maintained that all the accounts of the Stalinist show trials were nothing but a bunch of lies. I had such blind faith in the party that I couldn't imagine that anything of the kind had actually happened. However, as the result of a few minor incidents that I personally witnessed, even in Moscow, I began to have doubts about the democratic nature of the regime. I recall how we marched across Red Square on May Day. Although people were singing, I chose for some reason (I can no longer remember why) not to sing. A German female member of the party who was marching next to me asked me all of a sudden, "Why aren't you singing?" I couldn't think of an answer. As ridiculous as it sounds, this exchange led to a

brouhaha within our delegation. I considered the matter triv-
ial, unnecessary, and petty—certainly not a reason to be
expelled from the party.

Ironically, I was expelled from the Communist Party at the
very time I was working in the underground. The occasion
was a trip to England. My fellow party members told me to
keep my mouth shut and not to speak in public while visiting
England. However, an opportunity presented itself to talk
about the practices of the Nazi regime. I was asked to describe
conditions in Germany. Upon returning to Holland I was
reprimanded for having spoken at a meeting, something I had
been explicitly forbidden to do. All I had done, though, at the
meeting in Croydon, which had been organized by friends of
mine, was talk about the educational system in Nazi Germany, something that anyone with even a modicum of knowledge about the situation in Germany could have done as well.
In any event, I had "in petit bourgeois fashion placed myself
outside the ranks of the party."

At first I was terribly hurt at having been expelled from the
party, but as time went on I recovered and told myself that it
was their problem, not mine. A fellow party member in Holland, Wilhelm Knöchel (1899–1944), a member of the Central
Committee of the KPD and head of underground operations,
helped console me: "Have a little patience and bide your time
until the war. It'll all work out." He was later arrested, tried,
sentenced to death, and executed.* Knöchel was a worker
from the Ruhr. It wasn't until long after the war, when he was
already dead, that I learned his real name. We knew him as
"the old man"; he was my most important liaison within
the party.

After I returned to Holland from Moscow in 1936, I found
my family waiting on my doorstep. My parents and both my

*On Knöchel, see Beatrix Herlemann, *Auf verlorenem Posten: kommunistis-
cher Wiederstand im Zweiten Weltkrieg: Die Knöchel-Organisationen* (Bonn: Verlag Neue Gesellschaft, 1986). Wilhelm Knöchel used Amsterdam as a base to
carry out operations inside Germany.—Trans.

brothers had used semiofficial channels to get out of Germany and had been forced to leave all their possessions behind. They were headed for America but had to stay in Holland for a few months until their visas were processed. Until the processing was complete, my whole family lived near me in a rooming house, enabling us to have frequent get-togethers. In the course of the next several weeks, my elder brother Manfred, who was seventeen at the time, decided to stay with me in Holland. He hoped to continue the technical training he had begun in Hamburg. We found a slot for him in a technical high school. I was to watch over him while my parents created a secure livelihood in America. Even though they didn't agree with his decision at first, Manfred was determined to remain with me; we both loved each other very much. He ended up living in a typical student's room not far from me and quickly learned Dutch.

Manfred passed his exams after three years' study and then embarked for America via Le Havre on one of the last ships to leave Holland before the German invasion.

He came to visit me every Saturday and was crazy about Holland; that's where he met his first girlfriend. A short time earlier Manfred had seen the Nazis impose increasing restrictions on our father and witnessed Father trying desperately to find professional opportunities outside Germany. He even tried to emigrate to Egypt, but all his efforts were in vain. After being prohibited from participating in the national health-care program, Father was forbidden to employ "Aryans" to assist him in his medical practice. The only resource available to him was the Jewish Hospital. He was forced to relocate his office to his personal residence and was no longer allowed to treat non-Jews.

The first time I saw my father cry was when my parents left to go to America in 1936. "I know this is the last time I'll ever see you," he told me. He was very much a *German* Jew and couldn't make sense of what was happening. He was deeply depressed and angry, since his whole world had collapsed.

He passed the licensure examination for foreign medical school graduates in the United States, where he subsequently opened a practice and worked at Bellevue Hospital in New York City. However, he died soon afterward of a heart ailment. He simply couldn't take the pressure.

Both my brothers settled in America. Manfred became a successful engineer. He patented a number of inventions and worked for various companies, eventually becoming a computer consultant. He has retired in the meantime and has a son and daughter. My younger brother Robert became an anesthesiologist. He has a large family, and his children have children of their own now. Neither of them ever considered returning to Germany after the war. They became Americans.

I became a Swiss citizen before the Germans invaded Holland in May 1940 by marrying a Swiss; it was my first marriage. I took my husband's surname and was thereafter known as Ruth Stock. My first husband was an architect. I met him at a congress in Amsterdam. At first we wanted to marry in Switzerland, but the Swiss immigration authorities found out there was a warrant out for my arrest in Germany and deported me. So we married in Holland instead. As a Swiss citizen by marriage I subsequently accompanied my husband to Zurich, where we lived for more than a year. I worked with him and other architects on a book about the relation between architecture and the means of production. Even though this was, strictly speaking, a marriage of convenience, Oskar Stock and I had a close relationship. He was a thoroughly decent man to whom I will be forever grateful.

In addition to the political situation, my relationship with Werner continued to trouble me. It was very hard at first to cope with the fact that we were separated from each other. Initially, he visited me on a regular basis, but as time went on he came less and less often. He always had to give a reason for leaving Hamburg, which wasn't always easy to do. I lived in Switzerland, then in Holland again, and Werner lived in Germany. We had arranged to go skiing in Austria, but he never showed up. He told me later that our relationship had become too "complicated" and that he had met someone else. He wanted to remain in Germany and took the easy way out.

I was too proud to ask him to join me in Holland. In fact, I expected him to come up with the idea on his own or at least to discuss the possibility. Perhaps I might have asked him not to come, but we never even got to the point of broaching the issue. When war broke out, it became impossible to meet. Werner married his girlfriend Rita despite his guilty conscience. They had several children together.

This was the greatest disappointment in my life. There I was, stuck in Holland and although I wasn't unhappy—in fact, I was actually quite content—I was nevertheless despondent over the denouement of our love affair. Clearly, Werner's feelings were different from mine at the time. Later, after the war, he felt guilty and wanted to begin all over again. During the Hitler years this other woman had represented a way out for him. He was intent on building his legal practice and took the path of least resistance. However, he never became a Nazi or a member of the Nazi association of lawyers.

I never thought that Werner's profession and career would someday become more important to him than our relationship. After the war, he severed his ties to the KPD and became a member of the SPD [Sozialdemokratische Partei Deutschlands, or Social Democratic Party of Germany]. He was elected chief administrative officer of the city of Lüneburg, then mayor of Ludwigshafen, and later lord mayor of Frankfurt. In Frankfurt he was made director of the Deutscher Städtetag (the German League of Cities) in 1964, shortly before his death.

During the early part of the Nazi period, Werner often came to see me in Holland, usually once or twice a month. Though the visits were costly and difficult to arrange, we always had a good time together. I became pregnant by Werner after I was already married to Oskar and had changed my name to Stock, so I decided not to carry the pregnancy to term. I didn't say anything to Werner at the time, since it was impossible to discuss such matters, even in a letter. Given the awkward circumstances and the fact that there was a warrant out on me, I didn't feel I could raise a child alone. Later, I felt terribly sad. I asked Oskar how he would have reacted if I'd

suddenly told him that I was expecting. He would have been
delighted, he said. I remember that I burst out crying, because
I had aborted the pregnancy partly out of consideration for
his feelings.

The next time Werner visited, I told him the whole story.
He was deeply saddened and said how much he would have
liked to have had a child with me.

Werner was often more frightened than I during these visits
to Holland, even though he always had some kind of acceptable documentation to legitimize his trip. Now, however, I
realize how truly difficult it was to travel to Holland under
the conditions that existed at the time. And since romantic
relationships depend on personal contact, they often break up
precisely because of circumstances such as these.

Werner always had a guilty conscience over the breakup of
our relationship. Mischa, his first child, was killed when an
unexploded bomb blew up in his garden after the war. Werner
interpreted this horrible accident as divine retribution. To
quote him verbatim: "I was punished because of what I did to
you."

While living in exile and under occupation and after sepa-
rating from Werner, I didn't want to tie myself down. Yet even
under the occcupation, in the underground and in an atmosphere pervaded by fear, there was always time for flirting, sex,
and love; however, whether I was in or out of love, I never felt
that I had to have a man.

I would like to have had children of my own, but fortunately so many children have become part of my life over the
years that I no longer think of it as a failing not to have had
my own—though I must admit that for a time I suffered terribly as a result of being childless.

✿

After the German Invasion

I was living in a room on Haringvlietstraat in a married couple's apartment the day the Germans invaded Holland. Early in the morning as the sun rose, I saw German paratroops drop from the sky. The date was May 10; the weather was glorious. The night before we burned every document and piece of paper that could possibly have put us in jeopardy. Similar small fires were burning throughout Amsterdam. It was a strange sight, and the stench of burned paper hung like a pall over the city.

The queen and her government went into exile, the former escaping to Canada, the latter to England. The Austrian Nazi Seyss-Inquart became Reich commissioner for the occupied Netherlands. The Germans immediately began issuing anti-Jewish decrees. On May 14 Jews were barred from participating in civil defense. Then they were prohibited from carrying out the ritual slaughter of animals. This was followed on October 4 by a law prohibiting Jews from being promoted or employed in the civil service. At the same time, government officials, artists, and so on were made to fill out a form in which they had to declare their "Aryan descent." Beginning in January 1941, Jews had to report for registration. The authorities imposed a general curfew on all citizens that extended from midnight to 4 A.M. In the case of the Jews, however, it began at 8 P.M. and ended at 6 A.M. Jewish businesses were officially registered and "Aryan trustees" appointed. Jews were ordered to wear the yellow star and were forbidden to leave Amsterdam, use public facilities, eat in restaurants, or stay in hotels. They were forced to deposit their entire liquid assets in a Jewish bank chosen for this purpose—Lippmann, Rosenthal, and Company—and permitted to withdraw only negligible amounts of money. The first deportations began in February 1941. In the fall, the first roundups took place in eastern Holland, and in 1942 they began in Amsterdam as well.

From the outset there was a great sense of panic among the émigrés. Many of them did not want to live under Nazi rule again and committed suicide, including my best friends, the Oetinger family. So many people took their own lives that there were not enough coffins in which to bury them. The dead were simply stuffed into bags.

I visited the Oetinger family the night before they killed themselves. I had located an American woman who was employed at the U.S. consulate and might have saved their lives, using its good offices to get the family safely to America. The mood in the Oetinger household alternated between hope and despair. I thought the news I was bringing them would raise their spirits. They had two children: the older one was about two years of age, the other was still a baby. The baby was standing in his crib and refused to go to sleep. Lotte Oetinger was extremely upset; she was afraid he had swallowed a lightbulb from a flashlight. She tried to find the bulb. If she didn't find it she was prepared to encourage the child to vomit. As I watched the family frantically searching for the lightbulb, I couldn't imagine they would ever commit suicide. They seemed to want their baby to live. The American woman at the consulate—an elderly lady who had survived the 1906 San Francisco earthquake—told me, "Bring the family over tomorrow morning at nine, and I'll take them to the consulate." I went to meet the Oetingers the next morning, but they were nowhere to be found. I became extremely anxious, fearing they might have taken their lives after all. I phoned their neighbor, Hans Kramer, and asked him to check at once. It was either May 12 or 13. He reported that everyone in the family was dead. They had done a thorough job, using both gas and poison. The children were seated on their dead parents' laps in front of the kitchen stove. Everything had been sealed with black tape to prevent gas from leaking into the stairwell. It was one of the most dreadful sights I've ever seen. I've always reproached myself for not having stayed with them. After all, they told me what they were going to do and had offered me their clothes and their money, but I simply refused to believe them.

The Oetingers' little boy had been ill the day before, and the pediatrician who came to their apartment to treat the child killed himself and his family in a similar manner. Looking back, I think that the contact between the Oetingers and the pediatrician strengthened the resolve of both families to take their lives. I myself never considered committing suicide, even though I was sure I wouldn't survive the war.

Since I had a Swiss passport, I, like a number of other Swiss, went to the Swiss consulate on May 10, 1940, the day Holland was occupied by the Germans. At first I planned to escape to Switzerland, but that proved to be utterly out of the question. The trains weren't running, nothing was running, and the consulate was besieged by throngs of desperate people. Many Swiss wanted to find out what was going to happen to them. They were terribly shaken; it was mass confusion. Dr. W. S. Lantz, a practicing attorney with his own law firm, was the honorary Swiss consul. The day I went to the consulate, he was away. He lived on the outskirts of Amsterdam in Laren near Hilversum; however, transportation between the various parts of the city was nonexistent. There were no trains and there was no chance of getting a car. The city was in a state of total chaos. I was surprised when one of the secretaries at the consulate asked me, "Do you think you could you help us out a little and set people's minds at rest? Just tell them that the Swiss consul isn't in at the moment, that he lives outside Amsterdam." I did what I was asked. When the consul arrived three weeks later, he looked at me and inquired, "Why are *you* here?" I replied that I was a lawyer, that I was originally from Germany but was Swiss by marriage, and that my husband lived in Switzerland. That's how I became legal assistant and secretary to Dr. Lantz.

Since he was both an attorney and a consul, many of those who were in desperate straits sought to engage him as their personal lawyer, hoping that he would be of help to them because of his private practice and his public office. That, of course, was out of the question, though we advised people as best we could. I studied everything regarding emigration, including how Dutch Jews had actually succeeded in getting out of the country, namely, in exchange for large sums of money.

In order to register the Jews, the Germans forced them to complete a questionnaire. A number of Jews asked me to help them fill out the forms for the German authorities. Since the forms were quite complicated, they also went to Dr. Lantz's office. I was opposed, however, to providing too much detailed information, because I felt the Jews were putting themselves at risk. They didn't realize the danger involved in supplying the Germans with so much information. All valuables owned by Jews, for example, were to be entered on the forms, thereby facilitating the Germans' access to Jewish property. With the completed forms in hand, the Germans would know everything about the Jews, including particulars about their families—whether they had relatives and, if so, where they lived. As a consequence, they could be subjected to blackmail. If someone had a brother living in South America, for instance, the Germans might force that person to request money from the relative living abroad. Since the Germans were in urgent need of hard currency and it was impossible for them to obtain any in Britain or North America, they exerted pressure on the Jews to get money.

To the Germans, South America was the last major source of foreign exchange. To us it represented a way to save Jewish lives. We began corresponding with Jews' relatives living overseas. The Germans would hold out the prospect of granting permission to travel to, say, Colombia in exchange for a given amount of money. We agreed to the Germans' conditions; however, they never received any money from us, and they never got a single pfennig as a result of my efforts. The only reason I corresponded with Jews' relatives living abroad was to establish a list of exempted Jews whose fate could be put on hold and so allow them time to find a place to hide and disappear. There were approximately sixty people on my list. We would inform the appropriate Nazi authorities, for instance, that a particular Jew would be able to procure the desired hard currency if the Germans would just leave him to his own devices. The amount a Jew had to raise to buy his freedom was, if I remember correctly, 100,000 Reichmarks "per head," or 160,000 Reichmarks per family. When the military police or representatives of Nazi organizations came to abduct Jews under cover of darkness, those who had contacted us were able to present identification of sorts to verify their place on one of Ruth Stock's lists of exempted Jews. It's all so difficult to understand now. The point, though, is that we saved people's lives.

Switzerland represented and safeguarded the interests of Britain and the United States in the Netherlands, as it did in other countries occupied by the Germans. I'm thinking, for example, of Carl Lutz, the Swiss consul in Hungary who saved the lives of a great many Jews. Lantz was cast from the same mold. He was deeply disturbed by the injustices that were being committed. He had grown up in Holland, and his physician-father had been a well-known director of the Boerhaeve Hospital in Amsterdam. Lantz was a man of unimpeachable integrity and did everything in his power to prevent the worst from happening. If there were the slightest chance of helping someone—for example, if a victim of persecution had been born in England or America or we had a chance to claim that he or she had been—Lantz would intervene and try to facilitate that person's emigration. I greatly enjoyed working with Dr. Lantz.

The way Dr. Lantz reacted when I finally told him about my past showed just what kind of person he was. Since I didn't want to get him into trouble on my account, I felt it was incumbent on me after a certain period of time to tell him that the Germans had issued a warrant for my arrest under my maiden name, Lilienstein. I was completely candid with him:

"If you want me to leave, I'll go." He replied, "I am the Swiss consul, and it is my duty to help Swiss and non-Swiss alike." Then he did something truly unique so far as Switzerland is concerned—he issued me a Swiss passport under my married name and deliberately omitted any mention of my maiden name. My problems continued, though. It wasn't enough to have a new passport, because I was still on file with the police under my original surname. So my friend Magda van Emde Boas contrived to have my name deleted from the police files, ostensibly because I was leaving for Switzerland. In addition, Magda located a woman with whom she had attended university and whose father was mayor of the town of Kortenhoef. On the strength of the passport I had received from Lantz, he was willing to register me under the name Stock. Clearly, it pays to have a lot of friends!

Like every other Swiss passport, mine went through the consulate's bureaucratic mill; it was officially recorded and given the proper stamps and seals. Everyone in the consulate knew that I had a genuine faked passport or, if you will, a faked genuine passport. I only mention this because of the repercussions that followed from that knowledge.

I went to Davos to ski over the Christmas holiday in 1942 and debated whether I should stay in Switzerland for the duration of the war. What helped me make up my mind— aside from the fact that Lantz wanted me to return to Holland in order to settle some important matters—was an incident that occurred in Davos. A German officer dressed in civilian clothes—he knew me from Holland, but I can't recall his name—began talking to me: "Tell me, why are you so interested in the Jews? You're Swiss, after all. You realize you're playing with fire. The game is over now. It's no laughing matter anymore. We're not sending Jews to tend the soil of Poland. We're talking about the Final Solution." "What exactly do you mean?" I asked, "What's the 'Final Solution?'" "Just what I said," he replied, "the *Final* Solution." That was the first I had ever heard the term, and I was shocked. What the officer said might be true, which is why I felt I could not continue to remain in Switzerland. I had to get back to Holland and warn the Jews, which is what I did. However, the Jewish council—or rather, the members of the council whom I knew—simply refused to believe me. They regarded me as a hysterical woman who only increased people's anxieties. I've never forgiven myself for not having been more aggressive and telling more people what I knew.

At the time, Davos was teeming with German officers on leave. At a party I was attending, one of the officers came over and asked me where I came from. I told him I was Swiss and that I was from Mastrils in the canton of Graubünden. Another German, a specialist in racial science, asked if—just for the fun of it—he could measure my head. "You have the classic measurements of a woman from Grabünden!" he said. Ironically, his misevaluation of my ethnicity gave me a sense of security throughout the course of the war.

Lantz died early in 1943 in Switzerland as the result of a skiing accident. I was in Holland at the time, though I had already used my passport to visit Switzerland. Since I was a lawyer, Lantz's heirs in Switzerland made me the trustee of his estate. In that capacity I was able to continue trying to save victims of persecution from the clutches of the Germans. "Exempted Jews," that is, those who were included on my list, were never arrested. Incidentally, this did not mean that other Jews were arrested in their place. When a person caught in a Nazi dragnet spoke up and said, "I'm exempted and here's the paper to prove it," the Germans didn't go and seize someone else instead. The upshot [of my efforts] was simply that fewer people were arrested.

Even after Lantz's death, the waiting room outside his office, which was located in the Texeira de Mattos Bank, was always filled with people. One day I saw a tall, heavyset gentleman sitting there. He didn't have an appointment but insisted on speaking with me anyway. He turned out to be C. C. Brummer, the director of the Polak & Schwarz Company, a manufacturer of topical medicines and spirits. He asked me to make a plea on behalf of the Jewish owners of the firm. Brummer was a highly intelligent, diplomatic man. He had worked in the Dutch colonies for a number of years as a tax specialist. Subsequently, I was able to help the family.

My efforts to save the lives of persecuted Jews even brought me into contact with high-ranking representatives of German business and industry in the Netherlands. I met several times, for instance, with Alois Miedl, who consistently refused to play an active part in Nazi organizations. Miedl involved himself at all levels and even put in a good word for certain individuals. He subscribed to the dictum "I'll decide who's a Jew." Conflicts arose between German businessmen and representatives of the NSDAP that could sometimes be exploited to the benefit of the victims of the Nazi regime. It was a dangerous but exhilirating twilight world . . .

Part of my life was perfectly legitimate; I was a "regular" employee of the late Dr. Lantz's law firm. Aside from my quasi-legal activities there, I was and had from the outset been in touch with the resistance. The Dutch underground organizations were a hodgepodge of every conceivable type of group. Invariably you were personally acquainted only with the members of your own small group. Among the various underground organizations were the *knokploegen*, strong-arm squads that carried out acts of sabotage such as raiding offices where food distribution cards were printed and then providing them to members of the resistance. One of my friends was a tall, blond Dutchman named Henk Jonker, who had dyed his hair black and worked in the resistance disguised as a female nurse. He later married Maria Austria. There were even underground groups that specialized in providing shelter for people in trouble. The smaller underground organizations operated largely in isolation so there wouldn't be large numbers of people who knew or could betray each other.

At one time information regarding the German defenses along the Dutch coast came into my possession—detailed lists of the number of German troops, their weapons, and so forth. We typed the data on small cards and cigarette paper and forwarded the information to England and the Soviet Union. Just a few people, however, knew that I had sent the information to the Russians.

As a favor to Wilhelm Knöchel, a veteran German Communist, we operated a clandestine transmitter from my apartment for some time. I lived in a lovely building that had formerly been occupied by Swiss tenants; the owners were from Liechtenstein, and the Swiss consulate looked after the duchy's interests in the Netherlands. It was on the second floor of the apartment that we installed a transmitter and sent coded messages. We had to do so with great dispatch and then immediately remove and hide every piece of equipment.

I was anything but perfect when it came to carrying out covert operations. Once, for instance, I was asked to bribe a Gestapo official. Through my connections to Polak & Schwarz I was able to get my hands on some liquor. Besides topical medicines and other alcohol-based products, the company distilled brandy. So I took a big bottle of cognac with me to the office of the Gestapo as an inducement to confirm the inclusion of several Jews on my exempted list. I realized I would have to offer the bribe at just the right moment, but I was so agitated and so tense that I missed my opportunity and returned home with the brandy still in my possession.

Once I even used my Swiss passport to enter the lion's den, the Reichssicherheitshauptamt (Reich Security Main Office) in Berlin, where I met with officials to have Jews exempted from arrest and included on our list. The meeting had been arranged by the office of Jewish affairs in The Hague. The name of the person with whom I met was Zoepf, a military officer, head of Bureau IVB4 and chief of the Sicherheitspolizei (SIPO, or Security Police) and Sicherheitsdienst (SD, or Security Service) for The Hague. The head office was located in a large red building on 8 Prinz-Albrecht-Strasse. I submitted a list containing the names of Jews who I could prove had corresponded in writing with South America in order to obtain money. I'll never forget the atmosphere there. It was

loud. Bottles of beer were lying about everywhere—some
people were obviously inebriated. In short, it was disgusting.

In spite of my outward appearance, it never dawned on
anyone that I might be Jewish. All they were really interested
in was obtaining hard currency. Naturally, I was afraid. They
all seemed so brutish and coarse.

I was forced to wait for perhaps twenty minutes, and I was
angry at them for letting me just sit there. Then two men sat
down opposite me, and I said my little piece: "If you exempt
these Jews, there's a good chance you'll get the foreign exchange
you need. If I were in your place, I'd seize the opportunity." I
acted as though everything was business as usual, simply one
of my duties as the trustee of the late Dr. W. S. Lantz, Swiss
consul and attorney-at-law.

After obtaining the exemptions in Berlin and returning to
Holland, I received a call from Frau Freilinghaus of the office
of Jewish affairs in The Hague: "Why don't you come on
over? We'd like to talk to you about how you're coming
along so far as getting money from the Jews is concerned."
When I arrived at her office, she said, "You're Swiss, aren't
you? We just received a message from the Reichssicherheitshauptamt in Berlin informing us that there's supposed to be a very
dangerous individual operating here whose name happens to
be identical to yours—Ruth Stock. The Ruth Stock in question is not a native-born Swiss, but a German named Lilienstein, a criminal who pretends to be helping Jews here. Have
you ever encountered such a person? You are acquainted with
the members of the Swiss community here, are you not?" I
was totally nonplussed. I replied that, yes, I ought to know
her, especially considering the fact that we shared the same
name. I feigned ignorance. She must have returned to Switzerland, I said, or I'm certain I'd know her. To this day I'm not
sure whether Frau Freilinghaus was trying to warn me or was
really as naive as she appeared. At any rate, I somehow got
out of the building. It was winter. I was wearing a gray fur
coat and was so upset that I threw up behind the nearest tree
and burst into tears.

The consular official who assumed Lantz's duties upon his

death was ultimately responsible for my being unable to continue working. Spycher, a native of Bern, falsely informed the
Dutch immigration authorities and the Gestapo that I had
forged my own passport. Clearly, he was afraid that my passport might cause neutral Switzerland to be dragged into the
war! It's hard to believe, but there actually were people like
that in those days.

Shortly after Spycher contacted the Dutch, agents from the
immigration bureau came to my office, which was located
one floor above the consulate, and arrested me. Everyone in
the consulate witnessed the event and knew that Spycher had
informed on me. As I was being taken to the immigration
office, I thought I was done for. But the agent was neither a
Mussert [*] man, that is, a member of the small Dutch fascist
movement, nor a German installed by the occupation authorities. I told him the whole truth—that consul Lantz had
issued me the passport and signed it in order to save my life.
The agent was sympathetic and disclosed the name of the person who had informed on me. He also told me that the
informer would not give up and that the matter would eventually be reported to the Germans. I returned to my office
above the consulate only to find everyone standing there
waiting for me. I had the feeling that there must have been a
terrible row between Spycher and the employees of the consulate in my absence.

I was able to continue working just long enough to get the
word out to all those who had entrusted themselves to my
protection that I myself would now be looking for a place to
hide and would therefore be unable to do any more on their
behalf. They would now have to use the escape routes I had
helped select for them or go underground. Sorry to tell, some
of them were arrested in spite of our efforts, though a number
of those with whom I was involved did manage to survive. In
the event, Dutch Jews occasionally worked together with

---

[*] Anton Adriaan Mussert, 1894–1946, was the founder and head of the Dutch
National Socialist Movement (National-Socialistische Beweging, or NSB) that
collaborated with the German occupation.—Trans.

German and Dutch Communists. In addition, a number of Jewish businessmen gave financial support to the Communist Party to help oppose the occupation of their country and the persecution of the Jews.

Realizing that the situation had become too dangerous for me, I went underground in 1943. I had a quasi-legal hiding place in Kortenhoef on the outskirts of Amsterdam, where I was officially registered under my new name. I wanted to burn my bridges to ensure that all my work hadn't been for naught.

On the morning of April 10, 1943, I was on my way to work when friends intercepted me at a corner to warn me that the Gestapo was searching my office and that of Sepp Lantz. Sepp was the twin brother of the late consul, and his office was located in the same building as mine. He knew about many of my activities and had always covered for me. Constant Cornelis Brummer had earlier arranged a place for me to hide, and so I was immediately able to go underground. My life in the resistance had begun; I was never again to enter my office or my apartment.

The first few weeks of my dramatic escape took place in several phases. First, I severed all my relationships in order not to put my friends at risk. Nonetheless, I always found people who were willing to help me.

Constant Cornelis Brummer facilitated the second phase of my escape. Those who put me up had no idea of the danger to which they were exposing themselves. No sooner had I arrived than they asked me whether I would like to go to a soccer game with them. I was flabbergasted and declined the invitation. My conscience bothered me for taking advantage of their kindness and putting them in jeopardy. The night I arrived, a German general had been assassinated on the very street on which I found shelter. As a result, every house on the block was searched from top to bottom. It was winter, it was freezing, and I had to go out on the balcony in my nightgown to hide. I left the next morning.

I made my way to the home of my friend Annemarie

Bakels. She was Dutch but had grown up in Switzerland. I had made her acquaintance while I was working for Lantz. She offered me her apartment to hide in. She lived in Pijnacker, which was located between The Hague and Rotterdam. Her husband was serving time in prison for helping to publish the underground journal *Vrij Nederland*. No sooner had I arrived than she phoned her in-laws to inquire whether they had sent the regular weekly parcel to her incarcerated husband. Thank goodness she made the call, because her in-laws' maid told her that the police had just left and knew that Ruth Stock was in Pijnacker. Annemarie was pale as a ghost after putting down the phone; she told me that the police were on the way and that I had to leave at once. I grabbed my handbag and winter coat. Just as I exited through one door, the Gestapo came in through the other. They arrested Annemarie and made her swear to notify the Gestapo the moment she heard from me.

The first thing I did was go back to the hiding place in The Hague from which I had just come. I had a problem, though, since my apartment was now swarming with Dutch officers who had been called up by the Germans but had chosen instead to go underground.

This is when I made the only serious mistake during the entire time I spent in the underground. I called the parish office in Etersheim on the former Zuiderzee, now IJsselmeer, to inquire whether they could hide me. The pastor's wife instantly replied in the affirmative and gave me precise directions on how to get to their place. However, the phone had been tapped and our call monitored. I had known the Protestant pastor in Etersheim and his wife, Hanni Schipper, for quite some time, since they had often provided aid to refugees. With great prescience they had offered to hide me the moment I made the inevitable slipup. This was the first time I took advantage of their offer. The pastor was a man of unimpeachable rectitude and integrity. There were many people like him in Holland at the time. His wife was very active in the underground. She hid Jewish children, including the children of resistance fighters. Her house was, in fact, overflowing with children. I had hardly set foot on the parish grounds that night when two squads of police, riding up in big sedans, descended on the house and began searching every inch of the premises while a Bible study session was in progress in the basement. Hanni concealed me at the last moment in one of those big Dutch wardrobes used to store winter clothing in the summer and summer clothing in the winter. It turned out to be the only wardrobe that wasn't searched! Through a chink in the door I made out an SS man in big black boots pacing back and forth. It was dark in the wardrobe, but the room was illuminated. I was quite shaken after they left, but at least I had survived. The Schippers conducted themselves magnificently.

Early the next morning Hanni accompanied me to the so-called blue streetcar that went to Haarlem and from there to west Amsterdam. I was never as utterly exhausted as I was after that night—I was dead to the world. I was in such a comatose state, in fact, that I went a stop too far. That's when it finally dawned on me that—damn it—I did know someone here after all. There was a German pastor and his wife with whom I had once worked to find hiding places for children. However, their house was now teeming with children, too. I was scared and pale as a ghost when I arrived at their residence. I wasn't sure whether the Gestapo had picked up my trail again. Frau Pollatz opened the door, gave me the once-over, and pulled me inside. "I don't know if I've given the police and the Gestapo the slip," I explained. "I don't want to put the two of you at risk." She tried to allay my fears: "Don't talk now. Just lay down and rest for an hour. We can discuss things later." I felt as though I had arrived in paradise—imagine, people saying things like: Come on in, rest a while, we'll talk later.

After spending two weeks with the German pastor and his wife, I regained some of my strength. While I was resting, they found three possible accomodations for me—one with a group of intellectuals in Amsterdam, one with some farmers in Friesland, and one with a Calvinist blast furnace worker in Beverwijk. I opted for the blast furnace worker.

❁

Life in the Underground

A Dutch woman from the resistance smuggled me into Beverwijk to meet my new family. Once again I had no identification papers and was terribly frightened, yet this was the family with whom I was to remain for the lion's share of my time in hiding—until after the war, in fact.

The people of Beverwijk had two main sources of employment: the local iron and steel works (the Netherlands' biggest) and the many glasshouses and large open-air fields where strawberries were grown.

The van den Burgs were devoutly religious Calvinists who regarded their efforts to help me as a divine duty [the idea being that God had assigned them the role of rescuer and that their faith obliged them to find expression in works]: "You were placed at our doorstep that we might take care of you." The woman of the house, Griet, was pregnant, so my first assignment was to help her with the household chores. She gave birth to a girl named Ingetje. Ben, the father, was a shift worker who operated a crane at the blast furnace in Ijmuiden, near the German line of fortifications southwest of Beverwijk. He was a wonderful, honest man who was active in the Christian trade unions and had even taken part in strikes. Then there was Fenny, the eldest daughter, who was seven, and little Ben who had just turned two in 1943.

It was not unusual in Holland to hire household help before and after the birth of a child. Now *I* was obliged to play the part of helper and take care of all the household chores, that is, wash the windows, prepare meals, look after

73

the children, and shop—so far as it was possible to do so. In time members of the resistance provided me with a new set of authentic-looking identification papers, and my anxieties gradually began to subside. "You're not in more or less danger than any of us now," Griet said. So I even started working for the two underground newspapers in town. Among other things, I monitored British news broadcasts for them. The radio was hidden in a closet. One of the newspapers was published by the Calvinists, the other was more in the nature of an information bulletin. I translated radio reports on the current political and military situation from English into Dutch, which were then duplicated for distribution. We lived from broadcast to broadcast.

My friends in the underground quickly involved me again in the work of the resistance. I had the reputation of being a skilled forger, a reputation that was really somewhat inflated.

I was quite candid with the family and told them exactly what I was doing, and they in turn shared my concerns. "If they find out I'm living with you, they'll shoot you, too," I said. "Never mind, we can deal with that," they replied. It's hard to imagine that people actually said such things. It sounds incredible, but that's the way it was.

I consider it my duty to mention that in spite of everything, life went on pretty much as usual. We laughed a lot, and we experienced the many joys and sorrows of daily living. We didn't sit around in a state of constant fear and mope. I don't want to leave the reader with a negative and misleading impression about what it was like to go underground and live with a working-class couple and their three little children.

Every day, of course, we listened to reports of the German retreat. Sometimes when I heard the German song "I Had a Comrade" being played on German radio in commemoration of those who had been killed in action, I took the words quite literally and felt happy. At the same time, though, I was torn, because it was human beings after all who were dying.

As time went on, I learned to behave like a real Dutch

nanny and maid, which meant doing the so-called *buitenboel*, the Friday ritual of sweeping the sidewalk in front of your home and cleaning your house inside and out.

I was in constant danger of being exposed. The head of the family that lived next door to us at 17a Cornelis Matersweg, for instance, was a member of the Dutch National Socialist Movement, a small political party that never captured more than 4 percent of the vote. He was fighting on the side of the Germans in Russia and had left his wife in Beverwijk to raise their children by herself. Our relationship with his wife was as dangerous as it was strained. We avoided at all costs starting any kind of row with her. If we had quarreled with her, I expect that everything would have gone awry.

Ingetje was slowly becoming a young girl, which was a sign of just how long I had been living in Beverwijk. Being a strict Calvinist, Griet had never told a lie. But one day she said to me, "I've got to have a talk with our neighbor, so she won't get any wrong ideas about your staying here so long." Griet contrived to meet her in the backyard while hanging out diapers. Then, as if confiding in her, Griet said, "Nel [my assumed name] wants to leave us. Couldn't you talk to her? She wants to go to Haarlem. I know she won't earn as much if she stays here, but I really need her. I've never really felt the same since having the baby." As I was leaving the house the next morning, the neighbor buttonholed me: "I understand you want to go to Haarlem." "Well," I replied, "I've been here quite a long time already." "Don't forget," she cautioned, "there's more to eat here than in Haarlem. If I were you, I wouldn't leave right now." "All right," I said, "I'll think it over."

When the Dutch Nazi family next door moved out, their apartment was turned into a brothel for German soldiers, who would often knock on our door by mistake. One day a German military policeman rang the doorbell and then started pounding on the door—we knew it had to be a German soldier. No sooner had I opened up than he was standing inside our apartment. "Who do you want to speak to?" I asked. "Is there a Corry Goers living here?" he demanded. "You must have the wrong apartment," I said. "For all I know he lives next door." I tried my best to speak broken German, but he was undeterred and walked straight through the living room into the kitchen. We just managed to hide the underground newspapers behind a photograph of the queen. A tall, pear-shaped woman—small on top, rounded toward the bottom—Griet positioned herself directly in front of the queen's picture and stood stiff as a poker. All I could think was, "Please don't move." "Something funny's going on here," the policeman barked. "What do you mean 'funny'?" I said. "A strange man in a uniform comes bursting into your place . . . " The incident ended with him asking me why I spoke such good German.

I explained to him that I had once had a German sweet-heart, which piqued his interest and prompted him to ask me for a date. "I'm Dutch," I told him, "I can't allow myself to be seen with someone wearing that uniform." "I can come in civilian clothes," he parried. "How about after the war," I said, "not just now." He got the point and took an apple out of his pocket. It had been so long since I'd seen an apple; the children didn't even know what an apple was. Finally, he shook our hands and even wished us the best. We collapsed in our chairs, unable to speak for several minutes.

Henceforth I had two families. Although I get along quite well with my own family—my brothers and my nieces and nephews—I actually know my Dutch family better. I know every one of the children; in fact, I helped raise them, sparking their imaginations and even getting them interested in the arts. Ben, in particular, is like a son to me. His eldest son, Ben Junior, my "grandson" as it were, is an exceptionally gifted young musician who has in the meantime become an oboist. Like his father before him, Junior works in the steel mill—in the personnel department. He is a natural authority figure. His older daughter Fenny went to Canada, worked as a nurse, and is now retired. Ingetje—the girl who was born when I arrived—died of meningitis after the end of the war. Hers was a terrible fate, one made more terrible still for me when Griet said, "The child was only sent to us so that we could give you refuge."

As in all Calvinist families, the name of God was uttered only during prayer. The family prayed and read the Bible every noon and evening. As Ben Senior lay dying after the war, I made him the deathbed promise that I would always look after his children. "Promise me," he said, "that they will never go hungry."

I had so many positive experiences in Holland that to this day it remains a very special place to me — a home away from home or perhaps my real home. As soon as I cross the border into Holland, I have a good feeling. It always seemed to me as if the Dutch were more open and more natural than other nationalities. The idea that every person's individuality and desires should be respected, even if they deviate from the norm, is more widespread in Holland than in many other countries. I continue to have a close personal and professional relationship with the Netherlands. I enjoy speaking the language, and I am acquainted with nearly all the publishers in Holland, many of whom are my friends and know the story of my life.

Six months before the end of the war, on September 5, 1944, Dutch resistance forces and Allied troops drove the Germans back across the main rivers of the Netherlands, permanently liberating the southern part of the country. We had gathered flowers in preparation for our own liberation; however, the subsequent battle turned out badly for the Allies. It's difficult to gauge the depth of our disappointment. In addition to the sudden military setback, there were also severe food shortages. September 5, 1944 has entered Dutch history as *dolle Dinsdag* (mad Tuesday). Even the occupiers had packed their bags in anticipation of imminent evacuation. Worst of all, though, we still had to face the so-called hunger-winter, or famine of 1944–45.

I first realized that the war was truly coming to an end when I saw German soldiers staggering across the street drunk. The strict discipline that had characterized the German military vanished overnight and demoralization set in. The next day it was all over. On May 5, 1945, the armistice went into effect. In Beverwijk the war went on for one or two days more because a German officer had barricaded himself in one of the German fortifications at Ijmuiden* and was intent on fighting to the last drop of blood.

When they came, our liberators wore the uniform of the Canadian Army. We had a rough idea where they were deployed and knew that it wouldn't be long before they freed us. In the morning I rode my bicycle to a farmhouse to get some milk. I had stuffed a newly printed underground newspaper into my shoe with an article calling on people to get ready for the Canadians to liberate them. I told the farmer that for once I wanted real milk, not the usual watered-down liquid, because we were about to be freed.

The Canadians were given an indescribable welcome by the local inhabitants, who used anything they could lay their hands on to greet them. Everybody stood in front of their house and cheered. I thought that nobody on the working-class street on which I lived had any idea I was in hiding; it turned out, however, that they all knew. People came over with their last piece of zwieback and a bit of brandy to say, "So we got you through this thing alive." It was a full-fledged celebration. And although I can't adequately describe it, the liberation is reason enough to keep the memory of those years alive—years spent living in cramped quarters and constant fear. The sudden unrestrained joy of being freed, of having a burden lifted, was more overpowering than anything I've experienced since.

Shortly before the end of the war, aid packages from Sweden containing white bread, powdered milk, and sugar were dropped over the Netherlands. We suffered terribly from hunger, particularly during the final winter of the war. Many people went to the countryside to trade silver for cauliflower. The only ones who profited from the war were the farmers.

---

*The fortifications at Ijmuiden were part of the Germans' so-called Atlantic Wall, which stretched along the coastline from the Netherlands to Spain to prevent an Allied invasion.—Trans.

The Swedes, incidentally, were allocated special zones in which to drop their packages. The entire operation went smoothly; the packages "fell" from the sky and were distributed in an orderly fashion; there was no pushing or shoving.

Although I had promised my host family that I would break off contact with old friends and acquaintances for the duration of my stay, I didn't keep my word. As we ran out of food and became hungrier and hungrier, I got in touch with the Polak & Schwarz Co. and met with C. C. Brummer, returning to Beverwijk with a bottle of cooking oil and a bag of flour strapped to my bicycle. "It's the right oil!" Griet exclaimed, tears running down her cheeks. She couldn't get over the fact that such commodities still existed, a reaction that I'll never forget.

We employed every possible trick in those days to get something to eat. For example, we used little homemade stoves to obtain salt from seawater, which we then traded to farmers in exchange for food. Incidentally, the room in which the process was carried out was filled with condensation, since the salt was obtained through a process of evaporation. The walls were covered with saltwater stains. Farmers needed salt when they slaughtered pigs. It became an accepted medium of exchange. Admittedly, we never received any meat in trade, although we did occasionally get a half-liter of milk or a head of cabbage. We could only dream about bread and fried potatoes.

Conditions in Amsterdam were much worse than those in Beverwijk. Long columns of people trekked through Beverwijk on foot, on wooden-wheeled bicycles, and in handcarts as they made their way from Amsterdam to the farms of Friesland and the north. Many of them collapsed due to hunger and the cold and never reached their destination. I personally saw starving people die as they tried to reach the farm country. Incidentally, after the war we discovered that the Germans had deliberately helped create the food shortage. Following the liberation, we found bunkers and storage rooms dug into the dunes where the Germans had hoarded provisions. They were stuffed with potatoes, bread, and flour. Whenever we discovered one of these larders, we felt like killing Germans. Much of the food had gone bad in the meantime and was spoiled. Besides food, we also found records and phonographs. I didn't see any books, though there was lots of liquor.

I stayed on in Beverwijk after the armistice. I was afraid that none of my friends in Amsterdam had survived the war. Ten days later I finally summoned up the courage to ride my bicycle to Amsterdam, though I kept thinking along the way that all my friends had died, that nobody there was alive anymore. Just before I reached Magda's apartment, I ran into Lore Heilbrunn, an old acquaintance of mine who was a German-Jewish émigré like me. "Are they all dead, Lore?" I asked. "They're alive and going to celebrate the liberation today," she replied, "and they're all waiting for you." I let my bicycle drop to the ground and flung my arms around her neck. I was in such high spirits that I started to clap. Magda's husband roared with joy and carried me across the threshold like a bride. Thank goodness so many of my friends survived. I was speechless. Magda and her husband were there, as were other Jewish and non-Jewish friends, Dutch people, Germans, and a Czech soldier from Prague, one of Magda's friends. Unfortunately, though, many who had gone into hiding were missing.

Amsterdam, especially the Jewish section of the city, had been heavily damaged, not by German bombs, but by looters. The old buildings had been gutted; all that remained were the roof beams, and in some cases even they were missing because people had dragged them off to use as firewood.

After the Canadians arrived, we were faced with the problem of determining which German POWs to release and which ones to keep behind bars. I helped interrogate German officers. It was a fantastic feeling, no doubt with an admixture of malicious joy. The Canadians were extremely fair. They were followed about a week later by the British. One of the reasons I was involved in the interrogations was that I spoke excellent English, in addition to Dutch and German, of course. My knowledge of languages proved very useful in helping to solve crimes. For instance, the Germans had carried out executions right up to the liberation. However, we didn't know at the time exactly who the culprits were, but as a result of my interrogations we were able to establish the identity of the perpetrators and have them sent to prisoner-of-war camps. I still remember seeing a column of German soldiers being marched through the streets of Beverwijk and feeling not the slightest sympathy for them. My only thought was how young they all were!

We maintained contact, of course, with good Germans, for example, the soldiers who kept watch on and guarded the downstream gates of the sea locks at Ijmuiden. Having made common cause with us, they prevented Amsterdam from being flooded. The North Sea Canal extends in an east-west direction between Amsterdam and Ijmuiden on the North Sea with its three great locks. Together with Germans who, like us, were opposed to the war, the resistance damaged the locks to such an extent that the gates could no longer be opened. If we hadn't done so, the Germans might have inundated Amsterdam before retreating. In fact, they possessed plans to do exactly that.

I quickly established excellent contacts with the British. When I wanted to inform my mother, who was living in America, that I was still alive, it was only through the British military that I was able to wire my Aunt Päuli, my mother's youngest sister, who was living in England. Aunt Päuli then relayed my message by wire from Manchester to the United States.

The British regularly allowed me to ride with them between Beverwijk and Amsterdam. In return we supplied our British friends in Amsterdam with strawberries from Beverwijk, which was glutted with the fruit. When the British went home on leave, they would in turn bring back whatever we needed—bicycle tires, sweaters, etcetera.

Since I didn't have any sugar in my system [*sic*], I had a high tolerance for alcohol. I could drink any soldier under the table. We had a great time because the Tommies would show up with enormous quantities of liquor. They also brought us gasoline so that we could operate our vehicles.

Events of a more serious nature, of course, occurred as well. One evening, for instance, a friend of mine came over and insisted that I immediately go with him to the prison at Schoorl aan Zee. A member of the resistance had taken revenge against a Dutch Nazi by placing a hot iron on his behind. "It's our duty," my friend said, "to go and explain to him that such actions won't be tolerated. There will be no torture and no vigilante justice regardless of how angry a person feels." We drove to the prison together.

This was perhaps the best time of my life. All of a sudden we had regained our freedom; we no longer felt oppressed or threatened. It was simply incredible. In fact, I wouldn't mind experiencing that sensation again.

The fact that I had reestablished contact with my Aunt Päuli in Manchester only added to my feelings of joy. I loved her ever since I was a child, from the time she ran the two shoe stores in Bad Ems. I used to visit her there when I had personal problems. I even went to see her when I was a young woman to discuss the problems I was having with men. She knew Werner Bockelmann and Karl Olbrysch—all of my close boyfriends, in fact—and always kept abreast of my activities. She was forced to leave Germany because she was Jewish, a circumstance she regarded as a particular injustice in light of the fact that her German-Jewish husband had fought and died for Germany in the First World War. She moved to England and then emigrated to Israel after the founding of the Jewish state when she was already an old woman. Whenever I visited Israel, I would stay with her in Haifa. She died at ninety-four, and to the very end we argued over Israeli politics.

When the war was over I worked for a while in Holland, first in Beverwijk for the so-called Volksherstel (public relief agency). The Dutchmen who had been sent to Germany as forced laborers gradually returned. Because of the dislocations caused by the war, however, their families often no

longer resided in the same locality. The Volksherstel sought to
reunite families. Again my knowledge of German, English,
and Dutch proved most useful.

After my stint with the Volksherstel, I worked for the
Dutch firm of Polak & Schwarz until 1948. I did a great deal
of traveling during that period. I even took a trip to America
to visit my mother.

Mummy lay seriously ill in a New York hospital, and I
drove directly from the airport to see her. I found her lying in
a huge, oppressively hot hall with many other patients. Then
something incredible happened: when I encountered the doctor on call, I discovered that he was an acquaintance of mine
from Hamburg, Dr. Fritz Epstein. He helped me find a better
room for Mummy.

At the same time, I learned that my brother Manfred had
served with the U.S. Army and that his unit had been sent to
Italy. He had searched for me throughout Europe, but to no
avail. Not until later did he discover that I had survived the
war. After the war we found out little by little what had happened to the other members of our family. My mother's three
brothers had emigrated to Palestine in good time and survived. My father's only sister, Helma, and her husband were
gassed at Auschwitz. My father had two brothers as well. One
brother, Uncle Alfred, went into hiding in Paris; his children
were active members of the Résistance. He came through the
war alive. The other brother, Uncle Otto, was caught by the
Germans and killed. Most of the immediate members of my
father's family were murdered by the Nazis.

My family's fate shows just how lucky I was. I am infinite-
ly grateful to a great many people—to the Dutch family that
placed itself in great jeopardy and got me through the war and
to the many other people whom I have discussed in the course
of these pages.

My marriage to Oskar Stock, to whom I owe so much, was
annulled after the war. The annulment became a matter of
great urgency to him, since he had fallen in love with Eva

Maria Rosenberg and was planning to marry her. Incidentally, all three of us continued to remain friends. Eva became well known under the name Eva Maria Borer and for a number of decades was the editor in chief of the Swiss women's magazine *Annabelle*.

I was so overcome by emotion after the liberation that I was completely oblivious to political issues, for example, the future of Germany. All I remember is that to the extent that I was still a Communist, I was dissappointed that there hadn't been a revolution in Germany. Another opportunity missed. In a certain sense my protracted stay in Holland was spent in anticipation of the revolution in Germany. The division of Germany was not yet discernible. It was an occupied country. People had no idea how things would turn out. But one thing was certain: the occupation of the eastern part of the country by the Red Army was no substitute for a revolution.

❁

Hamburg after the War—Heinz Liepman

When during the winter of 1945–46 I was finally able to enter Germany legally again, the first city I visited was Hamburg. I had been sent there by Polak & Schwarz, the Amsterdam company for which I worked, to ascertain how the firm's plants in Germany had fared during the war, in particular the plant managers installed by the Nazis. The manager of the Hamburg plant, for example, had simply vanished . . .

I was introduced to Heinz Liepman while I was staying with my oldest friends in Hamburg, the Lüdtkes. I had just finished washing my hair and still had a towel wrapped around my head when he walked in.

I told him that I knew him by sight from before the war but hadn't really given him a second look. To be more precise, he was involved with the Bund proletarisch-revolutionärer Schriftsteller (Federation of Proletarian-Revolutionary Writers) with which I, as a member of the KPD, was also associated. At the time I thought of him as a typical example of the stereotypical pale, sickly Jew—the kind of Jewish recluse whom, if the truth be told, I loathe. Later on, however, I found him fascinating. He was something of a genius—astute but unassuming. He regarded working with words as both a pleasure and a pain, that is, he was a real writer.

When I met him in Hamburg he had already been back from exile in America for quite some time and was working as a freelance writer and journalist for German and other newspapers. He told me about his extensive correspondence with former Nazis and their reaction to his hard-hitting series of articles about the dangers confronting postwar Germany. He had attacked the so-called chameleons, ex-Nazis who now considered themselves pillars of the new Federal Republic. The letters, which unfortunately no longer exist, were filled with insults and threats of violence. I was eager to read them because I didn't really know what conditions were like in Germany.

Before the war Heini, as I called him, had been, among other things, the artistic director of the Hamburg Kammerspiele (Studio Theater) and a feature writer for the *Frankfurter Zeitung*. Subsequently he wrote several prize-winning novels that were translated into various languages. After going into exile in 1933, his books were burned by the Nazis. Before returning to Europe after the war, he reported on Germany for *Time* and other magazines. For many months after his return to Europe, he still used the English interjection "well" when speaking German. While living in exile he anglicized his surname Liepmann to Liepman.

Heini was an outstanding journalist and wrote for the newspaper *Die Welt* and the magazine *Kristall*, among other West German publications. He developed his own system for distributing his pieces to newspapers in various parts of Germany so that there was no overlap in his readership. Dr. Georg Ramseger, the editor of the feature section of *Die Welt*, was utterly convinced of the high quality of Heinz's work. We became good friends outside of work, and I still socialize with him and his wife today. Later, Heinz also wrote for the Dutch paper *Allgemeen Handelsblad* and became the correspondent in Germany for other foreign newspapers as well, in some cases using a pen name. He always worked as both a journalist and a writer and never felt there was any conflict between the two professions.

Soon after he returned from exile in America, the stories he had published in the U.S. appeared in Germany under the title *Das sechste Fenster im 11. Stock* (The sixth window on the eleventh floor, 1948), later reprinted in a number of magazines

and school textbooks.* He also worked for North German and
West German Radio.

One of the real reasons for my returning to Hamburg was
to see Werner again. I knew that he had married and had two
children. He and his wife spent New Year's Eve 1945 at the
Lüdtkes'. He wanted me to go with him to Lüneburg . . . I
vacillated for a while, but then said no. It was vintage Werner:
on the one hand, he wanted to separate from his wife, and on
the other, he didn't. I had no intention, however, of letting
anything destroy my growing love for Heinz.

The fact that Heinz was a morphine addict—and had been
for many years—was not easy to deal with. But I was pig-
headed enough to believe that he would give up his habit once
we lived together. He had become an addict early in life. Suffering from a painful kidney ailment, he had been given an
injection of morphine by a doctor. Heinz later told me that
after that first injection, he knew he was addicted. "The shot
did the trick, it freed me from the pain—but I knew I was
going to become an addict." And that is precisely what happened. His book about drug addiction was published in 1950
in the United States under the title *Case History* and in Germany in 1961 as *Der Ausweg: die Bekenntnisse des Morphinisten Martin M.* (The way out: the confessions of the morphine
addict Martin M.). It contains a number of autobiographical
allusions.†

Since I was deeply in love with Heinz, I felt certain that I
could cure him of his addiction. Throughout my life I
believed that I could accomplish any goal I set myself.
Though Heinz did much better for a time, I can't say he was

---

*Heinz Liepman, *Das sechste Fenster im 11. Stock* (Berlin: Der Neue Geist
Verlag, 1948).

†Heinz Liepman, *Der Ausweg: die Bekenntnisse des Morphinisten Martin M.*
(Reinbek bei Hamburg: Rowohlt, 1966); *Case History* (New York: Beechhurst
Press, 1950).

completely rehabilitated. That didn't happen until many years later.

We were married in 1949 in my hometown of Mastrils in the canton of Graubünden. I was Swiss, after all, and remained so even after my divorce from Oskar Stock. Alice and Rudolf Berman from Liechtenstein and an official from Chur to whom I had explained the tangled story of my past witnessed the marriage. I had known my friend Alice Berman in Holland, where she was an active member of the German-Jewish underground. Alice and Rudolf had two lovely children—Michael, with whom Heini had a marvelous rapport, and little Eveline.

In Hamburg and in Germany in general I had a privileged position owing to the fact that I was on assignment from my Dutch company and had received travel authorization from the Allied authorities. I also had plenty of ration coupons and could get all the meat, bread, and other provisions I wanted. I arranged to have food sent to Werner and his family in Lüneburg, since I knew they didn't have much to eat. I could get virtually anything I needed—from pins to cigarette lighters to food—at the central Allied exchange. I was living with the Lüdtkes at the time. When I first visited them, I carried a huge sack filled with goodies that were unattainable in Germany at the time.

In the course of one of my trips from Amsterdam to Germany, I lost any illusions I still had regarding the Communist Party. I was accompanied by Ida Falkenberg, the Dutch wife· of a German Communist. Although I had been expelled from the party, I still maintained contact with Communists well into 1945. Ida's husband, Otto, was an active member of the party in Dresden. Since it was impossible to travel to Germany and move about freely without official approval, I obtained papers for Ida to accompany me as my secretary, which was no easy task.

In Dresden Otto Falkenberg introduced me to a Russian apparatchik who tried to interrogate me. I didn't answer any of his questions. His methods of interrogation were ludicrous. For example, he would say, "You better talk now, because we're going to get it out of you anyway." I asked Otto why he had exposed me to a person like that. "He's from the Russian party," Otto said, "and can't help himself. All of these guys have been corrupted from working in the Soviet apparat." During the years following my expulsion from the party, Knöchel kept on telling me, "Don't worry. They'll rescind the expulsion order right after the war. No problem." However, after my encounter with the Russian apparatchik, I never again became a member of the party.

I saw Bodo Uhse again in Berlin after 1945. He had changed, and it was difficult to talk to him. He had a high position in the writers' federation in the Soviet zone of occupation and was living the life of a rich bourgeois enjoying lots of what were considered luxuries in those days. His Mexican wife went horseback riding every day. They lived outside the city in a fenced-off and secured housing development where many of the most popular writers of the future East Germany resided. What amazed me at the time was that there were such enormous social differences within the party.

Shortly after moving into Heini's apartment in Hamburg, we brought my mother over from America to stay with us. She had suffered a mild stroke and needed a lot of care. She lived with us until her death in 1956. Heini got along splendidly with her, perhaps because his own mother had died when he was very young. Since his father had also died when Heini was still a child, he was orphaned at a very young age, and he and his sister were raised by an uncle.

At first we lived quite simply in a furnished room on Schlüterstrasse. Later we moved to a lovely flat in Ohlstedt in a house with a sod roof. Then we moved to a top-floor apartment in one of the high-rises on Grindelallee.

Though the postwar period was fraught with problems, it was also a very interesting time in which to live. We often went to the theater; Heinz was a drama critic, after all. He taught me a great deal about the theater and literature. And I in turn introduced him to the fine arts and architecture. Maybe it was because we opened each other's eyes to so many beautiful things that we had such a happy marriage.

This was also the time when I began my career as a literary agent. Let me give you some background. When Heini decided to return to Germany from America, his U.S. publisher and his agent told him to scout around Germany to see whether any important writers had been overlooked because of the war. He therefore spoke with a number of German publishers; however, they for their part were much more interested in English and American literature. Fortunately, Heini had brought along a light-blue carbon copy of a list of books and authors for which he had been allowed to negotiate the sale of translation rights. The list contained, among other publications, Norman Mailer's *The Naked and the Dead,* J. D. Salinger's *The Catcher in the Rye,* and works by F. Scott Fitzgerald. Heini held exclusive rights to represent a number of U.S. publishers, including Doubleday.

The challenge of dealing with authors and publishers appealed to me instantly, and since Heini was really more interested in writing, he gradually handed more and more of the business over to me. Initially, we tried to find German publishers for English and American authors. Later, I expanded my activity to include other countries as well, for example, the Netherlands. Incidentally, Heini never earned as much from his work as a literary agent as he did from his journalistic assignments.

Before I began working for the agency, I was simply a housewife and Heini's personal guardian, not to mention his foremost critic. I never viewed the role of guardian as a burden. In fact, I enjoyed it, especially when it became clear that Heini's morphine dependency was beginning to subside.

It became clear to me over the years that people rarely overcome drug addiction through treatment programs alone. They always have to discover the underlying psychological reasons that caused them to voluntarily enslave themselves in the first place, because addiction is a form of slavery. After a number of unsuccessful attempts, Heini's case finally responded to psychotherapy, and nobody was happier than Heini himself.

The support that Heini and I received from good friends was of crucial importance. Willi Wulf proved to be my greatest help. Whenever I was afraid that Heini might start taking morphine again, I spoke with Willi and he would spend whole nights talking and drinking with Heinz and in this way prevent him from resuming his drug habit. Willi was Heini's best friend. He was a seaman, an expert on ships and seafaring who had learned his trade on the old sailing ships. Heinz had met him after the war through Willi's wife, Irma Lissauer. Irma was Jewish and had worked for the Hamburg Jewish Community for a number of years, both before and during the war. It was her responsibility, for instance, to notify Jews that they had been "selected" for deportation and tell them the date on which they were to be shipped out. Willi helped her go underground and provided her with food ration cards and hiding places. To be on the safe side, he also supplied her with a gun.

Willi's identification with the fate of the Jews went back to a traumatic experience that he told me about only after my persistent prodding. Once, after going on shore leave during the war, he heard shots ring out. He and a buddy went to investigate and saw a group of Jews digging their own graves. "What's going on here?" he asked the soldiers who were standing about. "We're shooting Jews," they answered. "What have they done?" he inquired. "Done? They're Jews," the soldiers responded. Willi swore that he would report what he had seen to Jewish Community officials so that they would counsel Jews not to follow orders issued by the German authorities. It was through his contacts with the Jewish Community that he met Irma Lissauer, who became his wife after the war. Heini had met Irma before 1933.

Willi and Irma are both dead now. I delivered their funeral orations.

A minor postscript: Irma wanted Willi to be buried next to her in the Jewish cemetery in Konstanz. However, the Jewish authorities declined her request because Willi wasn't a Jew. Nevertheless, I saw to it that both of them had their final resting place there after Irma's death.

❖

The Literary Agency

When I first returned to Hamburg in 1945 and met Heini, he told me about his experiences as an author in America. Like many other writers, he had discovered that authors were in a relatively weak position vis-à-vis publishers. And he had also learned that a professional literary agent could be of great assistance in representing an author and helping him protect his rights when negotiating a contract. At the time I didn't even know there was such a thing as a literary agent. But being a lawyer, I immediately wanted to find out more, and it wasn't long before I got the hang of the business.

The first books we represented sparked my instant enthusiasm. I found Norman Mailer's *The Naked and the Dead* to be an outstanding antiwar novel. And I was captivated by the literary quality and refreshing new tone of J. D. Salinger's *The Catcher in the Rye*. *The Catcher in the Rye* was first issued in German by a small Swiss press, Diana, in part because we couldn't get a percentage of the royalties in Germany. Incidentally, the novel didn't become well known in the German-speaking world until Kiepenheuer & Witsch published Heinrich and Annemarie Böll's translation.

Marketing foreign literature to German publishers was a difficult proposition, since Germans weren't allowed at the time to transfer money abroad directly. We frequently negotiated a book contract with three different publishing houses — a Swiss, a German, and an Austrian. The German-language book market was not a single entity as it is now. Each publisher paid a separate advance. And since the German state had been placed under Allied control, the Swiss were obliged to pay U.S. publishers any advances offered by German and Austrian publishers.

In Hamburg we worked with the following houses: Rowohlt, Krüger, Hoffmann & Campe, and Claasen. Hoffmann & Campe was Heini's publisher as well. Their senior reader was an elderly gentleman from the Soviet occupation zone; he was erudite, devoted, and an absolute bibliomaniac. When he came to see us, he would arrive carrying an enormous pile of books, and when he left, he would depart lugging another huge pile of books. H. M. Ledig-Rowohlt was already at the helm of the Rowohlt firm, working together with his father, Ernst Rowohlt. Ledig was a brilliant publisher and has remained a close friend over the years.

Even in those days I felt that the agency should be international in scope and facilitate universal access to important books from every corner of the globe. This goal was and continues to be my guiding vision. Heini, though, always thought the idea was a little wacky.

We found our secretary, Gertrud Schaefer, through the help-wanted ads. She introduced herself to us by saying, "Though I suppose you won't take me on, I simply have to tell you the truth: I was a gung-ho BDM girl."* I was so impressed by her honesty that I immediately hired her.

As a result of Heini's involvement with the world of literature and journalism and the rapid growth of the agency, our apartment became a cultural meeting place in the Hamburg of the 1950s. I can say without exaggeration that our home was a halfway house for everything cultural that was going on in Hamburg at the time. Though it may sound boastful, I can't think of any other way to put it.

For instance, we knew Hans-José Rehfisch (1891–1960) and his wife, Toni. My first meeting with them took place on

---

*The Bund deutscher Mädel, or League of German Girls, was a constituent organization of the Hitler Youth. —Trans.

the day their ship arrived in Hamburg from America, where they had been living in exile. Heini had given me background information on them beforehand. We quickly became the best of friends. Hans-José Rehfisch had been a well-known playwright during the pre-Nazi period and sought to reestablish himself in Germany after the war.

All four of us once attended the premiere of Carl Zuckmayer's play *Das kalte Licht* (The cold light, 1955). Following the performance we went down to the theater restaurant. Heinz and Rehfisch didn't think much of the play, and we felt rather uneasy about meeting the author. When Zuckmayer showed up radiating optimism, Rehfisch whispered to us, "Let me handle this." With a twinkle in his eye, he grabbed Zuckmayer with both hands and cooed in his ear, "Zuck!" We were saved.

We often got together with Peter Bamm (1897–1975), of whom we were extremely fond. In fact, we had a permanent circle of friends that besides the Lüdtkes included a number of actors and other individuals involved with the theater, cinema, and radio, including the Ramsegers, Wolfgang and Elli Krüger, and Hilde and Eugen Claasen.

Heini wrote news features for the radio in those days, like the one he did on Israel entitled "Die Früchte des Kaktus" (The fruits of the cactus). I believe he wrote it in 1956, after he and I had visited Israel for the first time. He had been given the assignment by Alfred Andersch, head of the radio essay department of South German Radio. It was a fascinating experience to talk with people who were building a new country in the middle of the desert. Except for a few relatives, Aunt Päuli among them, we saw very few of our former acquaintances. On the other hand, we made a number of new friends, including the architect Konrad Wachsmann (1901–80) from America, whom we met through mutual friends during a lecture tour in Israel. Wachsmann was originally from Germany and had lost his sister and mother in a concentration camp. We became fast friends as well as the agent for his book *Wen-*

depunkt im Bauen (English translation, *The Turning Point of Building: Structure and Design,* 1961).*

The first postwar German literature that I truly enjoyed was the work of Alfred Andersch. In fact, I wrote him after reading his book *Kirschen der Freiheit* (Cherries of freedom, 1952).† He was the first German-language author I felt like representing, so I suggested to him that we market his book abroad. One day he showed up at our front door in Ohlstedt. As it happened, Heini wasn't home at the time. "What a nice surprise to meet you like this," he said. "I've been invited to Hamburg to work for the Third Program [of North German Radio] and am looking for an apartment here." Our next-door neighbors and friends, the Zentners, had just moved to Munich. So in less than an hour I was able to get Andersch an apartment—no mean accomplishment in those days! And quite a service for the agency to perform.

For many years afterward we were next-door neighbors and good friends. Andersch's wife, Gisela, was an artist, and I was very fond of her paintings. Andersch was an extremely reserved, crusty, and somewhat irascible man, but nonetheless a good friend. I found a publisher for his book in France. After that I stopped representing him and merely offered him advice, since our families were too intimate [to mix business and friendship].

There was always something going on in the Andersch household. They each had children from previous marriages as well as having children together. They loved each other very much and had a good marriage. He was ecstatic about his wife's creative work, even to the point of writing about it. Later, when the Andersches moved to Switzerland, they would always find us a place to stay in Ticino, the city in which they lived, because they wanted us to be close to them.

---

*Konrad Wachsmann, *Wendepunkt im Bauen* (Weisbaden: Krausskopf-Verlag, 1959); *The Turning Point of Building: Structure and Design,* trans. Thomas E. Burton (New York: Reinhold, 1961).

†Alfred Andersch, *Kirschen der Freiheit* (Hamburg: Claasen, 1952); English translation included in *My Disappearance and Other Stories,* trans. Ralph Manheim (Garden City, N.Y.: Doubleday, 1978).

Andersch's principal interest was politics. Before the war he had been a longtime leader of the Communist Youth League in Munich. He rebelled early and with great fervor against his politically reactionary father. To his own children, whom we dearly loved, he was a very stern parent. I recall a story about the superintendent of our building, a wino. We kept a crate for milk bottles outside our front door, and one day little Martin Andersch said to me, "Aunt Ruth, isn't it strange how your milk is always red?" "Milk is white," I explained to him. Later it turned out that the super had made a habit of stashing his wine bottles in our milk crate.

Heini and I regarded Andersch as one of the most important German writers of our time. We have a painting by Gisela hanging in our office; for twenty years it has hung on the wall facing my desk.

❖

Zurich

In 1961 we decided to move the agency and our residence to Zurich. Heini wanted to make a fresh start in a place where no one knew him and where he could prove his ability from scratch. For him that place was Zurich, and it was from there that he reported on cultural affairs for *Die Welt* (Hamburg), North German Radio, the *Zürcher Woche*, the *Tagesanzeiger* (Zurich), and the *St. Galler Tagblatt* (Saint Gall). He contined to work as a writer on the side. In 1964 he published his last novel, *Karlchen, oder, die Tücken der Tugend,* a picaresque tale about a patient who is confined to a mental hospital for treatment of his "abnormal" habit of telling the truth and who eventually succeeds in escaping. Karlchen's naïveté reflects some of Heini's own.

In Zurich the agency was first located downtown in the Altstadt (old town). Though it was quite noisy, situated as it was between the River Limmat and Niederdorfstrasse, the Altstadt retained the flavor of old Zurich. Our building was called Zum Paradiesvogel (the Bird of Paradise). When we were expelled, as it were, from the Bird of Paradise, I was really quite desperate, because running a literary agency means accumulating tons of books. Luckily we found a marvelous house far up the slopes of the Zürichberg, where the agency is located today.

Heinz lived for five more years in Switzerland until his death in 1966. During that time he worked without letup and with great energy, often from morning to evening, writing

books and articles. We adapted quickly and without any
problem to our new city and new country. Of course, I was
already very familiar with Switzerland from the years I had
lived there with my first husband, Oskar Stock. In the evening
we would get together with old and new friends in Nieren-
dorf. Weekends we often spent in a little house in Ticino that
we had bought from an inheritance I had received from my
mother. Heinz adored the house. This was where we enter-
tained Alfred Andersch (1914–80) and his wife, Gisela; Günther Weisenborn (1902–69) and his wife, Joy; Erich Maria
Remarque (1898–1970); Robert Neumann (1897–1975) and
his wife, Helga; and the many others who visited us from
around the world. Heinz died in Agarone as the result of a heart
ailment from which he had suffered for several years.

I've been running the agency under the present organizational structure for quite a number of years now, together
with Eva Koralnik and Ruth Weibel. And if there's anything
I'm proud of, it's the team we've developed. Eva was a transla-
tor and interpreter and intially had no interest in joining the
firm. She had originally been recommended to me by Rusia
Lampel, a well-known Israeli author of radio plays and young
people's books. Eva met Rusia in Israel, and Rusia subsequently let me know that she had found someone whom she
could highly recommend to help me in my business, namely,
Eva. It turned out, though, that Eva had no interest in working for a literary agency; she simply wanted to continue doing
translation. We had a cup of coffee together anyway, and she
decided to remain on a trial basis. In the meantime, she has
been with the firm almost thirty years. Ruth Weibel, our
"newest" partner, came on board later, but, as in the case of
Eva, still just a short time after Heini's death. Like Eva, she
came in for a cup of tea—and has been with us ever since.

All of us have more work than we can handle. The firm
now employs eight clericals. And what with authors' and
publishers' visits, complicated negotiations, nighttime reading, and frequent business trips, it's a hectic job just to keep
the office running on an even keel. However, the joy of finding
the right publisher for the right book makes it all worthwhile.

Eva, her husband, and their two children live in the same building as I do, so our personal relationship and the work of the agency are very much intertwined. The fact that we three women have found a way to combine our private and professional lives is surely one of the reasons for our close friendship with one another and the pleasure we derive from our work. For any literary agency, a dependable system of accounting and contract management is a sine qua non. Our bookkeeper, Jörg Stöckli, has been with us for nearly twenty years, and the humorous reminders he sends out to the royalty departments of publishers everywhere are both loved and feared. Jörg is a fast and highly reliable worker who claims that he has absolutely no interest in literature. And yet it once came to light that he himself is a writer. A strange bookkeeper indeed—and a fantastic individual.

In 1977 I delivered an address to the German Academy for Language and Literature in Darmstadt on the long unrecognized profession of literary agent and on the profession's origins in history. Most of what I said then holds true today. The work remains basically the same: an agent tries to find a suitable publisher for a book while representing the interests of his or her client, the author.

There have been some general changes in the business, though. Now when a manuscript is accepted, more thought is given to the international ramifications and to so-called subsidiary rights, for example, paperback rights. The sale of film and television rights has also grown enormously in importance.

Another critical change is the increasing importance attached to advance payments, a practice that came over from America. Publishers pay huge advances for potential blockbusters. We represent mainly U.S., British, French, and Dutch authors and publishers, acting as intermediary for their books in Europe. The owners of copyright generally have unrealistic financial expectations.

We have seen little evidence of the often lamented crisis in the publishing industry. Nonetheless, the situation has changed as a result of the many takeovers and the formation of media conglomerates. There have always been mergers, of course, though somewhat fewer perhaps in publishing than in other industries. Fortunately for us, publishing houses have, in spite of everything, been able to preserve their individual character.

The publishers that are of particular importance to us have remained more or less the same over the years. We have, however, added several interesting new houses with which we enjoy doing business, since we feel that small presses have an especially important function, that is, they have the courage to experiment.

It is doubtless no accident that the three major literary agencies in the German-speaking world are located in Zurich. First, it is easy to conduct international business there. And second, Switzerland has a reputation for stability, a quality that is highly valued by authors everywhere. Every literary agency has its own particular style. And we greatly respect and are on friendly terms with the other agencies in Zurich.

We represent a growing number of the German-language authors who prefer to use an intermediary rather than dealing directly with a publisher. In addition, we are agents for a number of non-German authors from around the world, including A. B. Yehoshua, Henry Slesar, Aleksandar Tisma, Ryszard Kapuscinski, Andrei Bitov, Ida Fink, G. L. Durlacher, Chingiz Aitmatov, Norman Manea, and many others. We owe much of our success to our international affiliations as well as to the fact that the members of our agency team are multilingual.

Eva takes care of French literature. One of her accomplishments in this area was the debunking of the myth among German publishers that French literature could not be successfully marketed in German-speaking areas. Benoîte Groult's *Vaisseaux du coeur* (Salt on our skin, 1988)[*] is but one example of the soundness of Eva's judgment; Groult's novel was one of the biggest best-sellers in Germany in recent years.

---

[*]Benoîte Groult, *Les vaisseuax du coeur* (Paris, Grasset, 1988); German trans., *Salz auf unserer Haut,* trans. Irène Kuhn (Munich: Droemer, Knaur, 1988); English trans., *Salt on Our Skin,* trans. Mo Teitelbaum (London: Penguin, 1992).

We are also the agent for a number of literary estates, including those of Erich Fromm (1900–1980), Norbert Elias (1897–1990), Anne Frank (1929–45), Ernst Weiss (1884–1946), and Robert Neumann (1897–1975).

I've often been asked what rewards I derive from being a literary agent. Let me try to put it this way: I believe that as nations come to know one another better, they will move in the direction of world peace. And they will get to know each other better by working together. Books, among other things, are an important part of the process. Since literature helps bring nations closer to one another, every truly important book, regardless of where it was written, should be considered as a possibility for translation.

Although I do not believe that the love of reading is disappearing, we are nevertheless working with passionate commitment to make sure that that never happens—and we're having a lot of fun to boot. For years I've heard that television is replacing books, but I simply refuse to believe in the validity of that assertion. I think people will always be inclined to read.

Authors, Books, Friends

The greatest benefit and most interesting aspect of working in a literary agency are the often long-standing relationships with writers and publishers, relationships that I can't even begin to adequately describe here. A few reminiscences and anecdotes may perhaps indicate the various ways in which a relationship between an author and an agent develops.

The case of Heinrich Hannover is a good example. One of Heini's last projects was a book published by Rowohlt entitled *Kriegsdienstverweigerung: oder, Gilt noch das Grundgesetz?* (Conscientious objection to military service: or, Does the constitution still matter?, 1966). It dealt with the issue of refusing to fight in a war and was written together with Günter Amendt and Heinrich Hannover. Hannover is a lawyer who represented conscientious objectors at the time. We met him and his family while we were vacationing in the Black Forest. I happened to ask his children whether their father ever told them bedtime stories. They looked at him and beamed. He blushed slightly. When I asked Heinrich if he'd consider writing the stories down, he replied sheepishly that he already had and that the manuscript was tucked away in a drawer. He subsequently took it out and showed it to me. In the meantime, his *Pferd Huppdiwupp* (Hippety-Hop the horse) can be found in almost any nursery in Germany.

Our association with Arthur Hailey, whom we have represented since the publication of his first novel, began quite differently. I met him in London while I was visiting Doubleday, a client of ours practically from the moment we opened for business. As we were having breakfast together, Hailey said, "You look just like my American agent, and that's why I'd like you to be my European agent." Meanwhile, I've gotten to know his whole family—his son once stayed with us, in fact—though I've never managed to visit him on his yacht in the Bahamas.

With best-sellers such as *Airport*, *Hotel*, and *The Final Diagnosis* to his credit, Hailey is a classic example of the successful professional writer. He is an expert at constructing the perfect plot and spends at least two years researching each novel.

The case of Waltraud Anna Mitgutsch's novel *Die Züchtigung* (English translation variously *Punishment* and *Three Daughters*, 1987) is a different story again.* This is a powerful book for which I am particularly proud to have acted as agent. The author, who was living in Boston at the time, submitted the manuscript to a number of publishers and never received a reply. She was about to give up, when a friend took the manuscript and sent it to us on the off chance that we might be interested. I remember that the accompanying letter piqued my curiosity so much that I started to read the manuscript while it was still in the mail room and simply couldn't put it down.

That very same day I was entertaining Helmut Freilinghaus, the head reader for Claasen. I gave him the manuscript, and he called me the next day to say that he definitely wanted to publish it. However, I still hadn't met the author; nor did she know that her book had found a publisher. The news reached her on her thirty-sixth birthday.

---

*Waltraud Migutsch, *Die Züchtigung* (Düsseldorf: Claasen, 1985); *Punishment*, trans. Lisel Mueller (San Francisco: Harcourt Brace Jovanovich, 1987); *Three Daughters*, trans. Lisel Mueller (San Francisco: Harcourt Brace Jovanovich, 1987).

One of the most successful books we ever handled was Eric Malpass's novel *Morning's at Seven* (1966). I first met Eric in London. He told me that he was employed at a bank and was extremely unhappy working there and that more than anything else he wanted to write fiction. His first publications in Britain were short stories. They were followed by *Morning's at Seven*, which turned out to be a minor success in the United Kingdom.

I still recall how Rowohlt ended up publishing the German translation. I thought the book was terribly funny after reading it in English. A short time later Ledig-Rowohlt and his wife, Jane, came to visit us. They would often stop by our place on their way to some vacation spot in southern Europe. "I'm not sure this book is exactly up your alley," I told him, "but you might want to take it along for holiday reading. You'll get a real kick out of it." He and Jane continued on to St. Moritz. The next day Ledig phoned me to say that he wanted to acquire the translation rights immediately. He and his wife even came up with a title and asked me what I thought of it—*Morgens um sieben ist die Welt noch in Ordnung* (Mornings at seven all is right with the world).[*] The book was such a great success for Rowohlt that Malpass talked with his wife about leaving his job at the bank. The branch manager cautioned him: "Mr. Malpass, you'll have a pension if you stay with us. Are you willing to sacrifice that?" Indeed he was.

Even now, twenty-five years and twenty books later, when Eric calls, he'll ask me somewhat timidly, "Ruth, do you think there's another check on the way?" And I'll answer, "Of course." Then he'll ask, "How much do you think it's for?" It makes me feel good to know that I can always allay his anxieties.

Eric and Muriel visit Zurich every year, and we always have a great time chatting [and catching up on things]. Moral prin-

---

[*]Eric Lawson Malpass, *Morning's at Seven* (New York: Viking, 1966); *Morgens um sieben ist die Welt noch in Ordnung*, trans. Brigitte Roeseller (Reinbek bei Hamburg: Rowohlt, 1967).

ciples—people interacting socially and helping each other—
are particularly important to Malpass, and the little boy Gay-
lord, the main character in *Morning's at Seven,* is the finest
example of this aspect of his work.

I've always wondered why this novel became such a big hit
in Germany. Maybe it's because the Germans have no real
chance to raise their children in the unconventional manner
depicted in this wonderful book. Malpass does an excellent
job of describing how a father and mother try to understand
and bring out the best in their child. Clearly, the catchy title
was also a factor in making the book a success; the title has, in
fact, become a household word in Germany.

Sometimes agents are even—unintentional—matchmakers.
Eric's and Muriel's granddaughter Rosi worked for us as an au
pair girl and found the love of her life here, as did Cathy, the
sister of Malpass's British literary agent, who likewise worked
for us and married a Swiss.

On the other hand, my long friendship with the poet
Mascha Kaléko ended tragically. She was wearing a black cape
the day I met her many, many years ago in the waiting room
of the Rowohlt publishing house in Hamburg, when it was
still located on Hartungstrasse. It wasn't until later that I
became her agent and found publishers for her books *Horoskop
gefällig? Verse in Dur und Moll* (Would you like your horo-
scope? Verses in a major and minor key, 1979) and *Das himmelgraue Poesie Album* (The sky gray poetry album, 1968). [*]

Mascha was a dyed-in-the-wool Berliner. Her marvelous
poems made her a rising star in pre-World War II Germany.
As a Jew she was forced to emigrate, living in New York for a
number of years and later in Israel and Europe, that is, everywhere and nowhere.

One of her poems is especially dear to me:

[*]Mascha Kaléko, *Horoskop gefällig? Verse in Dur und Moll* (Berlin: Arani,
1979); *Das himmelgraue Poesie Album der Mascha Kaléko* (Berlin: L. Blanvalet,
1968).

MEMENTO

Vor meinem eignen Tod ist mir nicht bang,
Nur vor dem Tode derer, die mir nah sind.
Wie soll ich leben, wenn sie nicht mehr da sind?

Allein im Nebel tast ich todentlang
Und laß mich willig in das Dunkel treiben.
Das Gehen schmerzt nicht halb so wie das Bleiben.

Der weiß es wohl, dem gleiches widerfuhr;
—Und die es trugen, mögen mir vergeben.
Bedenkt: den eignen Tod, den stirbt man nur,
Doch mit dem Tod der andern muß man leben.

(No way at all do I fear my own death,
Though I don't want to be there when those close to me die.
Should I go on living when they are gone? Why?

Alone in the fog I grope toward death
And let myself drift into the darkness's source.
Going's less painful than staying the course.

If it's happened to you, you'll understand my song;
—And those who've been there, forgive my charades.
Remember: when you die, it's just you who've gone—
But when others expire you must live with their shades.)

I visited her in Jerusalem where she and her husband lived.
Chemjo Vinaver was a musician; Hassidic music was his life.
The two of them were a unique feature on the Jerusalem
cityscape—she, short with unruly black curls and scarlet lips;
he, tall, handsome, and white-maned. Mascha had a son,
Steven, whom she loved more than anything else in the world.
He was brilliant, wrote plays, and worked in America in the
television and movie industry.

One day Steven's agent in New York, Robert Lantz, wired
Mascha and Chemjo while they were visiting Zurich: "Mascha.

Come at once. Steven critically ill." As soon as Mascha arrived to be at her son's side, he died of pancreatitis.

When she returned to Zurich, she was utterly devastated and in a faltering voice told her husband what had happened. Then something peculiar occurred: they both became hysterical at the same time. "Lantz killed my son," Mascha screamed. "Are you crazy?" I said. "Lantz, who was so unselfish and looked after you and Steven?!" "And you're in cahoots with him!" she shouted at me. Strangely, her husband repeated her accusations word for word. They were both obsessed with the notion that their son's agent wanted to steal his idea for a play and that I knew about the plot. Lantz was a very decent person and had done everything he could for Steven and his parents. I was so distressed at the time by this incomprehensible turn of events and felt so helpless that I drove to Amsterdam to see Magda's husband, Coen van Emde Boas. I needed a psychiatrist to explain the situation to me. Coen told me that there really was such a syndrome, though I can no longer recall the name. Personally, I think that the reason Mascha and Chemjo idolized their son so much was that he represented a chance for them to redeem the hopes and dreams that had been dashed by Hitler. I was so hurt by their accusations that I asked them to leave my house and never saw them again. [Mascha died in 1975.]

Gisela Zoch-Westphal manages Mascha Kaléko's literary estate. One day she called me to inquire whether I would be interested in being the agent for Mascha's works. "I know Mascha would've liked it that way," she said. But I simply couldn't bring myself to do it.

We were on quite friendly terms with the writers who lived in close proximity to our house in Agarone. They included Erich Maria Remarque, Günther and Joy Weisenborn, Alfred and Gisela Andersch, Robert and Helga Neumann, Julius and Eva Hay, and later Erich and Annis Fromm.

Erich Maria Remarque (who was not a client of mine) and his third wife, Paulette Goddard, had a place on the shore of Lago Maggiore. Almost invariably when we visited them,

Erich would be seated at the piano playing. Erich called Heinz his only friend, but that was no doubt typical of Remarque's fondness for hyperbole. During the 1960s, Heinz conducted an interesting interview with Erich for *Die Welt* in which Remarque spoke very candidly about his life and his views on Germany.

Remarque was always nice to me, even though he was an insufferable snob. Erich loved to collect things, including women—a fact of which he was not a little proud. Indeed, he would talk about women as if he were showing off his collection of rugs. He had ten rugs piled on top of each other, one more beautiful than the next. He would fold back the end of one, for instance, only to reveal some fabulous Burmese prayer rug. He also collected paintings and rare sheets of music. He was one of the most generous people I ever knew. When he helped someone out, he would play the *grand seigneur*. He was very kind to me after Heini's death.

Joy and Günther Weisenborn were our closest neighbors in Agarone. Actually, we lived next to each other in Hamburg for many years and were already good friends back then. Günther was a well-known member of the resistance, and both he and Joy had served long prison sentences on account of their political activities. Günther wrote about this period in his memoirs entitled *Memorial* (1948) and in *Der lautlose Aufstand: Bericht über die Widerstandsbewegung des deutschen Volkes, 1933–1945* (The silent rebellion: A report on the resistance movement in Germany, 1933–1945; 1954).*

Joy accompanied me to Agarone to help with our move and was so taken with the surroundings that she asked Günther to join her. "As soon as he arrives," she said, "he'll want to stay here for good." It wasn't long before they bought the place below us. When Heini and I used to drive from Zurich to Agarone for the weekend with our poodle, Jeannie, it was almost as though we were living there as a pair of hermits.

---

*Günther Weisenborn, *Memorial* (Berlin: Aufbau-Verlag, 1948); *Der lautlose Aufstand: Bericht über die Widerstandsbewegung des deutschen Volkes, 1933–1945* (Hamburg: Rowohlt, 1954).

Even though Agarone is all built up now, it still seems like a resort to me. Part of the reason, of course, is Joy, who, along with Magda, is one of my very best girlfriends. She takes marvelous care of me, and we've grown even closer over the years.

Erich Fromm returned to Europe from his Mexican exile when he was already an old man and spent his final years in Locarno in the canton of Ticino. I always thought of him as a highly original thinker with a unique gift for presenting complex ideas in easy-to-understand terms.

I was introduced to Fromm by Felix Berner of the Deutsche Verlags-Anstalt, the house that had agreed to publish his complete works. Since the rights were widely scattered, for once it was the publisher who advised the author to contract with a literary agency.

At first our relationship was quite formal and businesslike. Whenever I visited Ticino for the weekend, I would always take tea with Erich and his American wife, Annis. As time went on, though, we became good friends. Erich was a marvelous storyteller and liked to sing Yiddish songs, which I greatly enjoyed hearing. Annis would try to teach me how to do some of the movements in t'ai chi. They were a delightful couple and very devoted to each other. They especially liked to eat gourmet meals and listen to music together. This was the only luxury that they allowed themselves. Otherwise they lived quite modestly in a cheerful modern apartment with a view of Lago Maggiore. I felt very much at home with them.

Fromm was raised in an Orthodox Jewish household, and his parents wanted him to become a rabbi. He told me how much effort it had required to free himself from the straitjacket of tradition. The decisive moment came when he dared to eat a piece of ham and realized that God wasn't going to send a bolt of lightning to strike him dead. In old age, however, Judaism became an important part of his life again.

Fromm's last work, which he completed in Ticino, was a collection entitled *On Disobedience and Other Essays* (1981).[*]

---

[*]Erich Fromm, *On Disobedience and Other Essays* (New York: Seabury Press, 1981); German trans., *Über den Ungehorsam und andere Essays*, trans. Liselotte and Ernst Mickel (Stuttgart: Deutsche Verlags-Anstalt, 1982).

It was also during this period that he was awarded the Nelly Sachs Prize. Since he was no longer able to travel, I read his acceptance speech for him. The speech stressed the importance in the lives of individuals and societies of having a guiding vision. To the very end, Erich exercised his talent for shaking people up and helping them to think and act for themselves.

We were also among the very first literary agents to represent African-American writers in Germany. One of my favorites was James Baldwin. Rowohlt became the publisher of his works in German translation. A character named Simple in the novels of Langston Hughes had already won that writer a devoted readership in the former East Germany. Finally and especially, there was Richard Wright and his book *Black Boy: A Record of Childhood and Youth* (1937; German translation, *Ich Negerjunge: die Geschichte einer Kindheit und Jugend*, 1947).

After reading the works of these black writers, I felt obliged to find publishers for them in Germany because of their high literary quality. By far most the interesting of the group, in my estimation, was Richard Wright. Time and again he wrote about the violent relations between blacks and whites, about rape and the victims of rape. When we showed him Hamburg and the Reeperbahn, he quickly renamed it "Raperbahn."* At the very beginning of my career as a literary agent, Wright helped me greatly to overcome my inhibitions and gave me self-confidence. He had written a radio play and asked me to act as his agent with North German Radio. I remember him saying as he accompanied me to the broadcast studio, "I won't even open my mouth. You do the talking. You make the decisions." His words of encouragement helped me enormously.

*The Reeperbahn—pronounced "Raper-bahn" in German—is a sleazy strip of clip joints, sex shows, and wholesale prostitution in the notorious Hamburg suburb of St. Pauli.—Trans.

In addition to writers of imaginative literature, scholarly authors were also important to me. For example, there was the Swiss art historian Konrad Farner, who had been denied a professorship solely on the grounds that he was a Communist. Applying Marxist categories to the arts, he wrote several fascinating studies. Farner and his family lived in Thalwil near Zurich. Because of his Communist affiliations, he was subjected to so much abuse and so many threats from his neighbors in 1956 [the year of the Hungarian revolution against the Soviets] that he was forced to abandon his home. Farner also wrote about the relation between Christianity and Communism. For political reasons alone I felt obliged to be his agent.

I was often a guest at the Farner home. Konrad was a real charmer. His wife, Martha, was a marvelous woman and the descendant of an ancient Swiss family. She could expand eloquently on the manners and customs of her native country. In fact, she published a book on the subject.

It must have been around 1960, during a visit to Amsterdam, that I happened to see a poster on Herengracht or Keizergracht announcing an exhibition of the works of Charlotte Salomon (1917–43). There were three rooms filled with her works. Painted on ordinary drawing paper, they were executed in vibrant colors and embellished with her own captions. As I looked more closely at the drawings, I realized that they shared a common theme—the autobiography of Lotte Salomon: her family; the tragedy surrounding her mother, who had committed suicide; and always again Charlotte; the Nazis; then her escape to join her grandparents in the south of France as refugees. The drawings in the sequence became increasingly frenetic, a kind of race against time, reflecting Lotte's own plight, for she was ultimately caught by the Nazis, taken away to Auschwitz, and gassed.

I was deeply moved by the power of the paintings and asked Lotte's father, the surgeon Dr. Albert Salomon, for permission to produce a book based on her drawings. The book came to fruition and coincidentally was my first coproduction. Kurt Wolff came to see us in Zurich and decided to bring out an American edition. Rowohlt issued the German, Bompiani the Italian, and Elsevier the Dutch edition. The book was printed in Japan.

Kurt and I sought to put together a biography based on her prodigious output—there were approximately a thousand [*sic*] paintings and drawings to choose from, all done in the last year of her life. I think we succeeded, and even now I am pleased with the results. In the meantime, Lotte Salomon's complete oeuvre has been published by Kiepenheuer & Witsch in a sumptuous catalog.

Without doubt one of our most important clients was the sociologist Norbert Elias (1897–1995). He wrote his magnum opus, *Über den Prozess der Zivilisation: soziogenetische und psychogenetische Untersuchungen* (English translation, *The Civilizing Process*, 1982), before the war, although it was relatively unrecognized at the time. In my opinion, his work provided a new and important approach to the study of sociology, even though the Marxist in me sometimes rebelled against it. In fact, that was precisely the criticism leveled at me by Elias. "There's still too much of the Marxist in you," he said.

Über den Prozess der Zivilisation was originally issued in 1939 by Haus zum Falken in Basle, a subsidiary of the Bern publisher Francke. *Die höfische Gesellschaft: Untersuchungen zur Soziologie des Königtums und der Soziologie der höfischen Aristokratie* (English translation, *The Court Society*, 1983) was published in 1969 by Luchterhand. Elias's big breakthrough, however, didn't come until 1976, when Suhrkamp brought out *Über den Prozess der Zivilisation* in a paperback edition. Since then Suhrkamp has been the publishing house for Elias's works, which have now been translated into thirteen languages.

I met Elias through Joop Goudsblom, a student of his and a professor of sociology in Amsterdam. Elias always called him "Jupp." He and other sociologists in Elias's circle asked whether I would take over the complicated international contract negotiations for Elias's publications.

Elias lived alone in Amsterdam and taught both there and

in Bielefeld. He frequently invited me to have dinner with him when I visited Holland. He very much enjoyed eating, and he ate well. I remember that even when he was a boy in the "Blau-Weiss" Jewish youth league, he was considered someone special, though I never mentioned that to him later. When he was a young man, he lost his sight in one eye as the result of a skiing accident and needed a special magnifying device in order to read. He was the kind of person who was absolutely convinced that his ideas and his ideas alone were the right ones. He felt very hurt that such a great injustice had been done to him as a result of war and exile, that it wasn't until late in his life that his ideas become widely disseminated, almost too late for him.

Elias was nearly a centenarian when he died, and even at the advanced age of ninety-three, he was the one who ultimately decided when his *Studien über die Deutschen: Machtkämpfe und Habitusentwicklung im 19. und 20. Jahrhundert* (English translation, *The Germans: Power Struggles and the Development of Habitus in the Nineteenth and Twentieth Centuries,* 1996) was ready to go to press.[*]

---

[*]Norbert Elias, *Studien über die Deutschen: Machtkämpfe und Habitusentwicklung im 19. und 20. Jahrhundert* (Frankfurt am Main: Suhrkamp, 1989); English trans., *The Germans: Power Struggles and the Development of Habitus in the Nineteenth and Twentieth Centuries,* ed. Michael Schröter, trans. and with a preface by Eric Dunning and Stephen Mennell (New York: Columbia University Press, 1996).

Epilogue

Now that I am eighty-four and can look back on my life with some perspective, I realize how often I got myself into nearly hopeless situations, how much suffering and unhappiness I witnessed, and how many of my friends did not survive the terrible persecutions perpetrated by the Nazis. When I ask myself why I didn't go mad living in such circumstances, I can only answer that I owe my survival to the many people everywhere whom I met in the course of my life, with whom I went to school and attended university, alongside whom I fought against the Nazi tyranny, who helped me when I myself was a victim of persecution, and who hid me and gave me the courage to go on. Since my childhood I have always been a person who had friends. I was very rarely alone or lonely. Whenever I was able, I helped myself, but when necessary I accepted help from others. That is probably why I never lost the will to live and always confronted new challenges with renewed optimism. I have always lived and worked with others—in Holland and at the literary agency, in Hamburg and Zurich. I still try to see all my friends (those who are still living), though I see some of them too rarely now, since they are scattered around the globe. I hope they are aware of how much I trusted them. This book is in essence the account of a person who was granted asylum during the darkest of hours, and in this sense it is a plea for solidarity among people.

❀

Historical Postscript

INGE MARSSOLEK

Memoirs provide us with information about contemporary history. Ruth Liepman's narrative is more than the record of her personal life—it re-creates history.

Ruth Liepman experienced World War I as a child. She saw firsthand wounded soldiers being treated by her father, an army doctor. She sensed the fear that her mother felt for her father during the war. Still, the war hardly affected her daily life. The battlefields were far away. The war was followed by the Revolution of 1918-19 that swept the empire of William II from the stage of history. In its wake the Weimar Republic, hated by Left and Right alike, was set up. Living mostly in Hamburg, Ruth Lilienstein passed from adolescence to young adulthood during the fourteen years of the republic's existence. The social, political, and economic crises of the time seem to have had only a marginal impact on the protected environment represented by her bourgeois parents' home. Nonetheless, the Liliensteins were aware of the social hardships that families, especially working-class families, suffered in a big city like Hamburg. Ruth's first encounter with the workers' movement was the May Day demonstration she attended in 1928. Even then the pending economic crisis with its mass unemployment was beginning to cast its shadow. Deeply involved in international trade, Hamburg was particularly affected by the Great Depression. The number of employed plunged by more than 50 percent in individual

branches of industry. In June 1933, 27 percent of white-collar
and 46 percent of blue-collar workers were jobless. Unlike
today, families faced hunger and poverty after just a few
weeks of unemployment.

By 1928 the KPD had already passed the peak of its ability
to attract artists and intellectuals. Nevertheless, such names as
Bertolt Brecht, Heinrich Vogeler, and John Heartfield were
still associated with the party. The radical nature of its program and its public image was particularly attractive to the
young. In the eyes of many, the Social Democrats had discred-
ited themselves by participating in the activities of Hamburg's
bougeois senate. The day-to-day drudgery of party work
must have been a disappointment in many respects to an idealistic young woman like Ruth Lilienstein. The KPD was
highly centralized and left little room for criticism or free
expression. The party wanted political soldiers—obedient and
conscientious to the point of self-abnegation. Between 1928
and 1929 the party made one of its many about-faces. Henceforth the Social Democrats were the main enemy, and the doc-
trine of "social fascism" determined Communist policy. In the
course of implementing this turnaround, the so-called right-
wing faction was expelled from the party—hence the so-called
war against the appeasers. The contacts Ruth Lilienstein established with the Salomon brothers and Bodo Uhse can be
traced back to the KPD's novel tactic of trying to win over the
followers of the NSDAP by using their, the Nazis', own
nationalist and socialist propaganda. Though the ploy was
largely unsuccessful, the party did manage to attract a small
group of national Bolshevik intellectuals and former Free
Corps members who had fought against the 1918–19 revolution. It is only now that we know that Ernst von Salomon had
for a time been in close contact with the KPD. Earlier he was
implicated in the murder of the liberal foreign minister
Walther Rathenau and was known as a nationalist. Throughout the Hitler years he remained a Prussian conservative and
kept his distance from the Nazis.

Though Ruth Liepman disapproved of the factional fighting and the harsh repudiation of the Social Democrats, she

seems to have been taken in by the cult surrounding the chair of the KPD, Ernst Thälmann, a native of Hamburg. "Teddy," as he was known, spoke frequently at mass meetings in Hamburg during this period, but nowhere does he appear in Liepman's memoirs.

The KPD had only a few intellectuals in its ranks. They remained mostly on the periphery and were given code names. It was felt that lawyers could be of more use to the party if their party membership did not become a matter of public knowledge. Ruth Lilienstein occupied a special position in the party hierarchy from the outset, not only because she was an intellectual, but also because she was a woman. She was able to maintain her freedom of action without the fear of being remprimanded. Ultimately, however, she was expelled from the party—while she was living in the underground, that is, at a time when the party in Germany had effectively ceased to exist.

It is clearly no acccident that from the beginning Ruth Liepman maintained contact with men such as Ernst Noffke in Hamburg and Richard Löwenthal (b. 1908) in Berlin who occupied important positions in the KPD's student organization. Ernst Noffke, by the way, survived the Stalinist purges and is reported to have worked with German prisoners of war in Russia on behalf of the Nationalkomittee "Freies Deutschland" (National Committee for a Free Germany).[*] Richard Löwenthal was expelled from the KPD in 1929. He was one of the most important theoreticians in the left-wing socialist opposition and the émigré community, especially in the Gruppe Neu Beginnen (New Beginning Group). After the war he taught at the Free University of Berlin's Otto Suhr Institute.

Hans Kippenberger, on the other hand, was a typical party functionary. The military apparatus that he built up and

---

[*]The Nationalkomittee "Freies Deutschland" was an organization founded on July 12–13, 1943, in Krasnoyarsk near Moscow by prisoners of war (mostly survivors of the German Sixth Army from Stalingrad), members of the Communist exile leadership, and antifascist writers.—Trans.

directed was an extension of the Comintern. The organization was largely independent of the Central Committee of the KPD and worked hand in glove with the GPU, the Soviet state security police. Jan Valtin (Richard Krebs, 1904–51) reported on the inhuman practices of the so-called M-Apparat and the GPU in his *Out of the Night* (1941).[*] He described how the KPD willingly sacrificed its own members. Like many other Communists, Kippenberger became a victim of the Stalinist purges.

As both a Jew and a Communist, Ruth Lilienstein was doubly stigmatized. The year 1933 could have been the beginning of a promising legal career for this twenty-four-year-old young woman. Of the 10,000 judges and public prosecutors in Germany at the time, only 36 were women. There were 14,683 male candidates for higher civil service and 990 female candidates. The evaluations Ruth Lilienstein received during her in-service training for the second state examination in law reveal that she was highly regarded as an attorney, even by her mostly conservative male bosses. And yet she was one of the first lawyers to be dismissed on "political and racial grounds." As early as March 14, 1933, she was denounced to the political police in Hamburg as a functionary of the KPD and as a Jew. Proceedings were subsequently instituted against her, and she was notified on June 21, 1933, that she had been discharged from her job with the Hamburg municipal government.

The possibility of being persecuted for working on behalf of the KPD was a calculated risk for Ruth Lilienstein in the Weimar Republic. Under the Nazi regime, she was almost instantly branded a "Jew" and a "non-German." Like other Jews, she was caught completely unprepared. In a statement, she tried to exploit the indecisiveness of the Nazi regime with regard to its treatment of World War I Jewish frontline fighters and so thwart the plans to fire her from her job with the

---

[*]Jan Valtin, *Out of the Night* (New York: Alliance Book Corp., 1941); German trans., *Tagebuch der Hölle: Aus dem Amerikanischen von Werner Krauss* (Cologne: Kiepenheuer & Witsch, 1957).

Hamburg city government. Her indignation comes through in her concluding sentence: "Finally, I would like to note that I can prove that my family has resided in the Rhineland since the thirteenth century." It was the nonreligious Jews in particular, that is, those who were instrumental in shaping modern German Jewry, who were incapable of grasping the murderous consequences of the Nazis' anti-Semitic policies. Like so many other German Jews, Theodor Lilienstein was forced to come to the agonzing conclusion that his Jewish heritage made it impossible for him to live in National Socialist Germany. He was allowed to practice medicine only within strictly defined limits. Already in 1933 most Jewish physicians were excluded from participating in the national health-care program. This action was just one of six hundred "special rulings" enacted even before the promulgation of the so-called Nuremberg Laws that were designed to exclude Jews entirely from German society.

Ruth Lilienstein's political activities were risky enough, but her ties to Karl Olbrysch, in particular, placed her in real jeopardy. Olbrysch went into hiding on February 28, 1933, the day after the Reichstag fire. The emergency decree that was promulgated that same day abrogated a number of basic civil rights and gave the national Reich government the right to assume police and other powers in the *Länder,* or state governments. As a consequence, the KPD was forced to go underground throughout Germany, even in cities like Hamburg, where the Nazis still did not form part of the local government. Olbrysch was arrested in June 1933 and sentenced on November 20, 1934, to a term of three years in prison. In 1938 he emigrated to England. He apparently intended to move on to Canada after Britain declared war on the Third Reich, but German naval forces sank the ship on which he was sailing.

In what was later referred to as the "model National Socialist *Gau* of Hamburg,"[*] the persecution of Communists and Social Democrats was conducted with exceptional cruelty. In

---

[*]*Gau* is an old German term for particular (tribal) regions. — Trans.

early April 1933, a concentration camp was set up on the grounds of the correctional facility in the Hamburg suburb of Fuhlsbüttel, the notorious KolaFu or Konzentrationslager Fuhlsbüttel, where SS and SA guards tortured and brutalized political prisoners, many of whom perished as a result. Under the direction of Curt Rothenberger, the Hamburg department of justice was integrated into the Nazi tyranny without a hitch. By the spring of 1934 the Gestapo had crushed the underground KPD in Hamburg in a series of two major operations and arrested their leading functionaries. Ruth Lilienstein escaped just in the nick of time.

Her job as a courier based in Amsterdam reveals that her assignments came from the KPD's "foreign directorate West" based in Amsterdam. So-called foreign directorates had been set up in 1934 by the recently outlawed KPD in the countries bordering Germany. Because of the nature of underground operations, the foreign directorates were relatively independent of the "domestic directorate" that the illegal party maintained in Berlin. Wilhelm Knöchel, code-named "the old man," had been ordered by party leaders living in exile in Moscow to go to Hamburg for several months and advise underground groups operating in the city. He was subsequently assigned to the foreign directorate West, where he met Ruth. Knöchel was a man of above-average intelligence. He was extremely skillful in dealing with his non-Communist allies and was regarded as an independent thinker.

After the Nazis occupied the Netherlands, German Communists as well as Jewish refugees were forced to go into hiding. At the same time, Knöchel tried to advance the date for his return to Germany so that he could rebuild the party's underground organization. Money was required in order to carry out these activities, and Ruth Lilienstein was an important fund-raiser. Using her connections with Communist organizations, she also managed to help Jews go underground and escape from Germany and the territories occupied by the Germans.

In 1942 Knöchel and his group succeeded in setting up a clandestine organization in western Germany. Their publication *Der Friedenskämpfer* (Fighters for peace) was conspicuous for its unusually candid appraisals of the condition and mood of workers inside Germany. The group was broken up by the Nazis in 1943 when Knöchel was already terminally ill. In June 1944 he and most of the members of his group were sentenced to death and executed.